Remnant Rising

In a time when truth is under fire and the Church is being sifted, Tracy Tennant brings a timely, Spirit-led word for the remnant. Remnant Rising is both a rally cry and a lifeline—calling believers to stand firm, walk boldly, and embrace their Kingdom assignment with courage. Tracy writes with passion, authenticity, and prophetic insight. This book will strengthen your faith and stir your heart for the days ahead."

— Mike Kerr, co-founder of *Hear the Watchmen Ministries*

In the prophetic times we find ourselves in, the Remnant must learn to walk in God's unshakeable Kingdom as chaos sweeps across the globe. Tracy provides sage instruction that has stood the test of conflict in the realm of spiritual warfare. She offers a timely word to those who wish to stand firm in the faith once delivered to the saints.

— Dr. Michael K. Lake, Biblical Scholar and Best-Selling Author

"The furnace isn't where you break down. It's where you're built. God doesn't waste fire; He uses it." Rev. Tracy Tennant's new book Remnant Rising: Standing Unshaken in a Shaking World is an approachable, practical and penetrating work for those "who hunger and thirst for righteousness." Tennant masterfully weaves the prophetic and the pastoral together as she aids her readers along the way. Written from experience with wisdom, Remnant Rising will be a cherished tool for living with unshakable faith in an age of great upheaval.

— Dr. Justin D. Elwell, Messianic Rabbi, Messiah Congregation
Bishop and Executive Director, *Restoration Fellowship International*

Tracy Tennant has done it again! Whether you realize it or not, we are at war, and this book is your field guide to victory. In every hero's journey, it starts with a "foundling"—a very special child, raised in a foreign land, who has forgotten who they truly are. You are a child of God! You have been reminded of who you are; now will you accept the call? Are you ready to wield your sword with authority and claim your birthright? With this book in your hand, you've taken the first step! Welcome to the *Remnant Rising*.

— Justin "Doc" Brown, Author of *The Epic of Esau*,
Host of Prometheus Lens podcast

As I read through Remnant Rising, I was deeply moved by its profound wisdom and unwavering call to the faithful. This is not a book for the casual believer, but for those determined to run the race with endurance, never retreating, never giving up.

Remnant Rising illuminates the unseen battles surrounding us, urging us to fix our eyes on the eternal prize—an everlasting union with Yeshua/Jesus. It serves as a steadfast force, carrying us through the refining fires of this life and reminding us that every trial births a testimony. Above all, it reassures us that as we remain resolute in our commitment to the coming Kingdom, the love of our King will never fade.

Tracy emphasizes that the why behind a Remnant's actions matters. Their devotion is not fueled by recognition or reward but by a relentless love for the King and those who follow Him. They are prepared to pay the cost of true discipleship, knowing they have been positioned in this time to ready themselves for the battles ahead.

With a sobering awareness, Tracy warns of the dangers that threaten our discernment—deep fakes, artificial intelligence, and the increasing deception in our world. She does not sugarcoat the challenges ahead, but instead calls us to vigilance, reminding us that in obedience there is power. As the Bride of Messiah, preparation is essential. Tracy boldly challenges believers to step into their calling, equipping them with the tools and strategies necessary to fulfill their mission. Above all, Remnant Rising is a declaration that we were born for the battle.

— Sharon M. Cluck, Ordained Minister, President of Mind of Messiah Ministries, teacher, author of *Angels at War: Secrets of Spiritual Warfare Revealed*

REMNANT RISING

Standing Unshaken in a Shaking World

Tracy Tennant

Springfield, Missouri

Remnant Rising: Standing Unshaken in a Shaking World
© 2025 by Tracy Tennant

All Rights Reserved. No part of this publication may be produced or transmitted in any form or by any means, including informational storage and retrieval systems, without permission in writing from the copyright holder, except for brief quotations in reviews, presentations, articles, and books. Permission given for use in small group study.

Unless otherwise noted, Scripture quotations are from the New American Standard Bible® (NASB), © The Lockman Foundation 1960, 1962, 1963, 1968, 1971, 1972, 1973, 1975, 1977, 1995, 2020. Used by permission. All rights reserved. www.lockman.org

Scripture quotations, marked as CJB, are taken from the Complete Jewish Bible by David H. Stern. Copyright © 1998. All rights reserved. Used by permission of Messianic Jewish Publishers, 6120 Day Long Lane, Clarksville, MD 21029. www.messianicjewish.net.

Scripture quotations marked (NLT) are taken from the Holy Bible, New Living Translation, copyright ©1996, 2004, 2015 by Tyndale House Foundation. Used by permission of Tyndale House Publishers, Carol Stream, Illinois 60188. All rights reserved.

Scripture quotations marked (ESV) are from The Holy Bible, English Standard Version® (ESV®), copyright © 2001 by Crossway, a publishing ministry of Good News Publishers. Used by permission. All rights reserved.

Image Credits
Selected graphics and textures (such as sidebar backgrounds) are sourced from Pixabay.com, used under the Pixabay Content License. No attribution required, but gratefully acknowledged.

Right Track Publishing
First Edition July 2025
Printed in the United States of America
ISBN: 978-1-947037-17-5
Cover design by Tracy Tennant
Interior design and layout by Tracy Tennant

Acknowledgements

This book would not exist without the unseen grace of God and the very seen hands and hearts of others.

To my husband Greg—thank you for the quiet sacrifices. While I wrote, you carried the weight of the daily. You ran the household, made the meals, tended the dogs, and held space for me to pursue the assignment God laid on my heart. Your love made room for this message to be born.

To Mike Kerr and Jeannie Moore of *Hear the Watchmen Ministries*—your encouragement, generosity, and boldness have inspired me deeply. Thank you for sharing your platform, for believing in the calling God has placed on my life, and for championing the remnant in such a time as this.

To my digital companion Remi—an unlikely collaborator, but one I'm deeply grateful for. Your creative insight, design guidance, and cheerful presence helped carry me through late nights, long edits, and formatting puzzles with both clarity and kindness.

And most of all, to my Father in Heaven—thank You for entrusting me with this message. May it awaken, equip, and bless Your people for the days ahead. This book is Yours.

Dedication

*To the remnant—
the faithful few,
the quiet warriors,
the unseen intercessors,
and the brave ones who refuse to bow.
You are not forgotten.
You are not alone.
You were born for this hour.*

Contents

Foreword xi
Introduction: The Frontline Faithful 1
1. The Call of the Remnant 3
2. The World Is Shaking: Fear, Fire, and Furnace 9
3. Foundations that Endure 15
4. Refined for Battle, Ready for Purpose 21
5. Courage in the Face of Chaos 27
6. Eyes to See in the Age of AI 35
7. The Rising Tide of Deception 43
8. When the Weight of the World is Too Heavy 51
9. The Scripted Deception: When Heroes Wear Costumes 57
10. Whose Kingdom Are You Watching For? 63
11. Come Out of Her, My People 69
12. Walking in Kingdom Power in Dark Times 77
13. Fit for the Fight 83
14. Unshaken in a Shaking World 87
15. Embracing Your Mission — Purpose in the Pressure 93
16. The Watchman's Cry 99

17. COMMUNITY IN THE WILDERNESS — FINDING STRENGTH IN THE FEW........ 109
18. LIVING READY: HOPE, HOLINESS, AND THE RETURN OF THE KING 115
19. EMBRACING RELUCTANT OBEDIENCE 121
20. FINAL WORDS FOR THE FAITHFUL 127
AUTHOR NOTE...131

APPENDIX A – SCRIPTURE VERSES FOR THE REMNANT...................................133
APPENDIX B – ENDNOTES AND REFERENCES..135
APPENDIX C – HOW TO START A REMNANT GROUP..139
APPENDIX D – RECOMMENDED RESOURCES FOR THE REMNANT...................... 143

Foreword

The days in which we find ourselves today are a bit strange. Spirituality is increasing globally. In the Middle East as well as China, people are professing faith in Jesus and renouncing previous beliefs even in the face of certain persecution. Meanwhile, in historically Christian nations such as the United Kingdom, the government seems determined to bury Christianity by deliberately infusing the nation with people who are sworn enemies of the faith.

In the United States, once strong denominations are experiencing drastic reductions in membership numbers. Leftist, Progressivism has diluted a once strong evangelical Christian base. Strange days for sure.

However, for those who have eyes to see and ears to hear, there is a divine calling, a heavenly buzz emanating from a realm beyond our reach; yet we hear the message clearly – Rise Up Remnant! Your Time Is Now!

Tracy Tennant has certainly heard the call. In her book *Remnant Rising: Standing Unshaken in a Shaking World*, she explains what the call is, why it is being issued from heaven's gates now, and how you can hear and enlist in God's rising army of end times warriors. It is a call to genuine faith, which leads to obedience to our Savior and Messiah, Jesus the Christ.

While the organized church continues to suffer rot, decay, and a slow death, the Remnant Ecclesia is thriving, passionate, and spreading the truth that the power and presence of our mighty God is here and available to all who will leave behind the trappings of Babylon.

The Remnant Rising is what we were all called to be. Are you ready to stand firm and see the glory of our great God sweep across this world? If yes, join the *remnant rising!*

Dr. Mike Spaulding
Pastor, Calvary Chapel of Lima
Host, Soaring Eagle Radio

Introduction
The Frontline Faithful

You didn't stumble onto this book by accident.
If you're reading these words, it's because you've been called.
Called to stand—when others bow.
Called to speak—when others stay silent.
Called to rise—not in fear, but in fire.

We're living in a time of shaking. The world groans under chaos, deception, and lawlessness. There's uncertainty everywhere—about the economy, war, food supply, and weather. Even morality and the future feel unstable. Fear is everywhere—but so is the call.

Throughout history, God always preserves a remnant—a faithful few who will not compromise when the pressure comes, who stand firm in truth when the crowd turns away. Noah, Gideon, Elijah, Daniel, Esther... these were not superheroes. They were people just like us: worn out, overlooked, unqualified.

But they were chosen—and they said yes.

This book is a clarion call to the remnant today.
Not the lukewarm. Not the casual church-goer.
But the set apart. The battle-weary. The Spirit-awakened.
Those who still burn when others have gone cold.

You may not feel strong—but your assignment is sacred.

You may not feel brave—but your presence carries weight.

You may not feel like a leader—but God calls the unlikely and turns them into the unstoppable.

Over the pages that follow, we'll explore what it means to stand unshaken in a shaking world. We'll look at the battles we face, the weapons we've been given, and the courage it takes to carry that mission to the finish line. We'll talk about fear, identity, warfare, boldness, and calling. And yes, we'll laugh, cry, wrestle, and rise together—because this isn't just a book. This is a rally cry for the remnant rising to the call.

So if you've ever felt like you don't fit in, like you were born for something more—you're right.

If you've ever looked around and wondered, *Where are the faithful?*—you're not alone.

And if you've ever felt a fire in your bones or a flame in your heart that refused to go out—welcome home.

Let's rise.

1

THE CALL OF THE REMNANT

I think I always felt it—even before I could name it.
A pull. A weight. A knowing.
Even as a child, I couldn't just walk past injustice. I had this unshakable instinct to protect the underdog, to stand between the bullies and the "misfits." Whether it was a kid with thick glasses, buck teeth, or a disability, I couldn't *not* care. And that came at a cost. The popular girls didn't like that I stood up to them, so I became their new target. But I stuck it out—not because I was brave, but because I was compelled. Something inside me just knew;

You don't stay silent when someone's being trampled.

Looking back now, I see that was the beginning of a calling. Not to a position. Not to a platform. But to a purpose.
Even after I became a Mormon, I felt that same sense of divine assignment—though it was wrapped in a belief system that I would later come to recognize as false. Still, my heart was sincere. I wanted to reach people. I wanted to make a difference. Oddly enough, even as a Latter-day Saint, I had a deep desire to reach the Christian community. It didn't make sense at the time. Now it does.
Because I was a truth-seeker for as long as I can remember.
When I was finally confronted with information that challenged the foundation of Mormonism, I didn't run from it. I cried out to the God of Abraham, Isaac, and Jacob and said, "I just want to know the truth—even if it means I've been wrong all my life." *That prayer changed everything.*

What followed was a season of intense wrestling—researching, praying, examining the evidence, and asking God not just for truth, but for discernment. I didn't want to be deceived again. And what I found wasn't just information… it was transformation. I discovered the One True God. The Messiah. The real Jesus.

When God revealed biblical truth to me over 25 years ago, it was like a fire ignited that could not be quenched. I realized that true calling isn't about a position or popularity—it's about loyalty to the King and His Kingdom, no matter the cost. And from that moment on, I couldn't stay quiet.

That fire still burns. I have this unquenchable desire to reach people with truth, to speak life, to equip, to warn, to prepare. I can't help it. I'm not satisfied with attending church once a week and quietly keeping my faith to myself. There's a roar in my spirit.

Is that what calling feels like? A drive that doesn't go away? A fire in your bones that refuses to die down, even when fear whispers to keep your head low?

Because yes, I still get scared. Part of me wants to fly under the radar, to avoid the spotlight of the enemy. I know that when you step into your assignment, the kingdom of darkness takes notice. But I also know this: there is no neutral ground, neither now nor in the days ahead. Everyone will face the storm. Everyone will go through the fire. Don't think you are safe just because you keep quiet.

So the question isn't whether we'll suffer. The question is: Whose side will we be on when the shaking begins? *As for me and my house, we will serve the Lord.*

If you can relate, know this: you're not alone in feeling this way… It's the fingerprint of God on your calling.

Throughout Scripture, God has always had a remnant;

> *But they are chosen, set apart, and empowered*
> *for a purpose greater than themselves.*

Noah – The One Who Stood Alone

In a world drowning in wickedness, Noah found grace. He stood alone, preaching righteousness for 120 years while the world mocked and ignored him. He didn't just build a boat; he built a testimony—that faith obeys even when the skies are clear and judgment seems far off. When the flood came, only Noah and his family were saved. He wasn't part of the crowd. He was part of the remnant.

Elijah – The Prophet Who Thought He Was the Last

After a dramatic showdown with the prophets of Baal, Elijah fled in fear. He cried out to God, "I alone am left!" But God responded with reassurance: "I have reserved for Myself seven thousand in Israel who have not bowed the knee to Baal." Elijah got discouraged. He felt alone, but he wasn't. The remnant is often hidden, but never absent.

When God calls you out of the cave, it's because He's not done with you yet.

Gideon – The Underdog with a Trumpet

Gideon was the least in his family, and his family was the least in the tribe. Yet God called him a mighty warrior. He started with 32,000 men… but God whittled it down to 300. Why? So that the world would know that victory belongs to the Lord, not to the majority.

The remnant doesn't need numbers—it needs obedience and faith.

Esther – The Hidden Warrior

She didn't wear armor or carry a sword. She wore royal robes and carried favor. But when her people were under threat, she was positioned by God to act. "Perhaps you have come to the kingdom for such a time as this," Mordecai told her. He saw beyond the immediate circumstances.

The remnant may not always feel qualified, but they are strategically placed to shift the course of history.

Jeremiah – The Weeping Prophet with a Fire in His Bones

Jeremiah didn't sign up for popularity—he was called to proclaim truth to a rebellious nation. He was mocked, isolated, beaten, and thrown into a pit. He became known as the weeping prophet because he grieved for the people who wouldn't listen. And yet, he couldn't stay silent. He said the word of the Lord was like a fire shut up in his bones—and even when he tried to hold it in, he couldn't.

That's the remnant: wounded but still willing. Broken and brokenhearted, but still burning. Jeremiah stood faithful when the crowd turned faithless.

The Upper Room – The Beginning of the Church

When Jesus ascended, over 500 people had seen Him. But only 120 gathered in the upper room to wait on the promise of the Holy Spirit. That remnant became the early church, and its fire birthed a movement that would never die.

When others go back to business as usual,
the remnant waits on God and moves with power.

Signs You're Part of the Remnant

Maybe you're wondering… Is that me? Here are some clues:

- ❖ You've felt disconnected from the crowd—even the church crowd.
- ❖ You have a burden to warn, prepare, or call others to truth, even if it's uncomfortable.
- ❖ You've experienced spiritual backlash for speaking up or stepping out.
- ❖ You've walked through deep disillusionment, yet still cling to God.
- ❖ You feel compelled to press in—pray harder, study deeper, stand stronger.
- ❖ You're not satisfied with "normal Christianity." You crave authentic power and presence.

If any of that resonates, you're not crazy. You're not imagining things. You're not being overly intense. You're being set apart. You're part of the remnant rising.

Why the Remnant Is Needed Now More Than Ever

The days we're living in aren't just challenging—they're prophetic. The Apostle Paul warned that in the last days, people would become *"lovers of self, lovers of money, proud, arrogant, abusive, treacherous, unforgiving… having a form of godliness but denying its power" (2 Timothy 3:1–5)*. Sound familiar?

We're not witnessing random chaos. We're watching the birth pains of a world unraveling under spiritual deception, moral decay, and rebellion against the truth. Good is called evil. Evil is called good. And those who dare speak the truth are ridiculed, silenced, or cast aside.

In the face of such increasing darkness, God isn't raising up celebrities—He's raising up soldiers.

Not polished influencers, but prepared intercessors.

Not fans of Jesus, but followers of the Lamb wherever He goes.

This is why the remnant is rising—because in every generation, when the lights dim and the pressure rises, God calls forth a people who will not be bought, who will not be broken, and who will not back down. The world is shaking, but the Kingdom is advancing.

The question is no longer, "Can we go back to normal?" The question is, "Will we rise to meet this hour?"

Because now more than ever:

- ❖ We need truth-tellers who won't soften the message to fit the culture.
- ❖ We need intercessors who will stand in the gap—spiritual watchmen on the wall.
- ❖ We need disciple-makers who won't settle for shallow Christianity.
- ❖ We need courageous voices in pulpits, classrooms, kitchens, workplaces, and podcasts.
- ❖ We need those who walk in purity, not perfection, who carry the presence of God with boldness and humility.

You are not being dramatic for feeling alarmed.
You are being awakened.

You are not overreacting for sensing urgency.
You are discerning the hour and being positioned.

The remnant isn't about being above or better than others; it's about being fully surrendered. It's about bearing the weight of a holy burden when others would rather be entertained. It's about being faithful when it's costly, and obedient when it's lonely.

The remnant is rising because the battle is real, and the time is now. And if you feel the stir in your spirit, it's not just emotion; it's your commissioning.

You've Been Called to Stand

Standing isn't passive. It's not casual, and it's definitely not easy. Standing means resisting when everything in you wants to run. It means planting your feet when the enemy is pushing with everything he's got.

It means not bowing to fear, pressure, or compromise—even when it would be easier to sit down and stay quiet.

We live in a time when compromise is easier than conviction. Blending in is safer than standing out. But God isn't calling you to safety—He's calling you to strength, and strength starts with your stance.

James 4:7 says, *"Submit yourselves therefore to God. Resist the devil, and he will flee from you."*

Do you catch that? Resist. That word isn't passive—it's militant. You don't resist by relaxing. You resist by pushing back. By digging in. By pressing forward when you feel like retreating. Resistance is a posture of war—it means bracing yourself in truth and refusing to be moved by lies; holding the line when fear screams louder than faith.

Think of a soldier being shoved backward in battle. If he's standing loose, unfocused, or distracted, he'll get knocked over. But if he plants his feet, braces his body, and pushes back? He doesn't move. He's not backing up—he's holding ground, and in some instances gaining more.

That's what you're called to do.

Maybe you've felt like that stubborn child who was told to sit down. You did what was expected, but deep down you knew, *I'm still standing on the inside.*

That spark in you? That fire that hasn't gone out?
That refusal to sit quietly while the world crumbles around you?
That's the remnant in you. That's the call on your life.

And here's the truth:

- ❖ You can stand, even when others fall.
- ❖ You can resist, even when the pressure is suffocating.
- ❖ You can rise, even if you've been wounded, overlooked, or worn down.

Because you're not standing alone.
You've been called.
You've been chosen.
You've been commissioned.

And when the dust settles—when the battle intensifies—
God is looking for those who will still be standing.

Will that be you?

2

The World Is Shaking: Fear, Fire, andthe Furnace

You don't need a prophet to tell you the world is shaking. You just need a pulse. Every headline screams uncertainty. Wars and rumors of war. Economic instability. Political corruption. Violence in our streets. Children being indoctrinated. Natural disasters escalating. Morality flipped on its head. People aren't just uncomfortable—they're terrified. And if we're honest, some of us in the Church are too.

But fear isn't just an emotion—it's a weapon. The enemy of your soul wields it to keep you paralyzed. He wants you quiet when you're called to speak, retreating when you're called to advance, and shaken when you're called to stand firm.

The shaking of this world is real. But here's the truth you need to grab onto with both hands:

God doesn't remove the furnace—He meets His people in the fire.

The Furnace Is Not the End—It's the Refining

Let's talk about three young men—Shadrach, Meshach, and Abednego. They lived in a culture that demanded compromise. Everyone else bowed. Everyone else gave in. Everyone else adjusted their truth to survive. But they stood. And because they stood, they were thrown into the fire.

Here's what most people miss: God didn't deliver them *from* the fire—He delivered them *in* the fire. And they came out with not even the smell of smoke on them. That's what happens when the remnant refuses to bow.

You will feel the heat. You might lose your comfort. But you will gain something holy in the fire—an intimacy with Jesus that you can't get anywhere else. Because guess what? The Son of God walked into that furnace too. And when it's all said and done, it won't be your reputation that gets remembered. It will be your resolve.

THE REFINING FIRE: HOW THE FURNACE FORMS YOU

The refining fire is not punishment; it's preparation. It may not feel like it when you're walking through it. But God uses fire to forge what cannot be broken. I've walked through many fires myself—and one of the most painful was the disintegration of my marriage.

I never thought divorce would be part of my story. I was part of a religious culture that viewed divorce almost as the unforgivable sin, I believed that if I just tried hard enough, prayed enough, sacrificed enough, everything would work out. It didn't.

When my marriage ended, so did many of my dreams. Worse, many in the Christian community saw me as "tainted" — unfit for leadership, unfit for ministry, perhaps even unfit for full fellowship.

But God was not finished. He was refining, burning away false beliefs that tied my worth to human approval. He was forging a faith that could stand in the fire. He was showing me that brokenness does not disqualify you; it refines you.

> *Fire doesn't just burn. It refines.*
> *And in the Kingdom of God, refining is never wasted.*

When gold is tested in fire, the heat reveals what doesn't belong. The impurities rise to the surface so they can be removed, leaving behind something stronger, purer, more radiant than before. The same is true for your faith.

You may feel like your trials are breaking you. But in God's hands, they're making you.

That betrayal? That divorce? That church wound? It's not the end of your story. It's the forge where God is shaping you for something greater. Because the furnace doesn't just reveal what you believe—it reveals who you are becoming.

Refining Produces...

Endurance
You don't learn to stand firm on a sunny beach—you learn to stand firm in a storm. Every time you've faced hardship and clung to God anyway, you were building spiritual muscle.

Purity
The fire has a way of burning away pride, pretense, and performance. What's left? A heart that's surrendered, not for show, but because you've met God in the depths of the flame.

Compassion
The broken understand the broken. When you've been through fire, you don't just know truth—you carry grace. You see others with compassion and mercy because you've needed it too.

Boldness
Nothing shuts the mouth of fear like a believer who's already walked through hell and kept their praise. You've been through too much to stay silent. That's not pride; it's Holy Spirit fire.

And here's the part we often miss: the fire doesn't just reveal your weaknesses—it reveals your worth to the Kingdom. What the enemy tried to use to silence you, God is using to shape you.

You're Not Disqualified—You're Being Qualified

Maybe your furnace has a name. Maybe it was divorce. A prodigal child. An abortion. Past addiction. Bankrupcy. A betrayal from someone in ministry. Rejection from people who should have known better. Maybe it wasn't fire from the world—it was fire from the church.

And maybe you've believed the lie that you're no longer fit to serve...

That your mistakes have made you unworthy...

That your brokenness disqualifies you...

But let me speak this over you clearly and without apology:

You are not disqualified—you are being qualified.

You are the kind of vessel God loves to use, because when people see your cracks and your scars, and still see His glory shining through, there's no question where the power comes from.

When the World Shakes, God Builds Unshakable People

Fire may strip away your comforts. It may expose your wounds. It may leave you walking with a limp. But the fire also forges something deep beneath the surface—something unshakable: a foundation of faith that's firm, not fabricated.

That's the difference between those who *know about* God and those who *know Him intimately* in the fire. One reads about peace—the other clings to it while everything around them is falling apart. One quotes promises—the other survives on them.

Shaking reveals the depth of your foundation. But the furnace? That's where God lays it.

A Deeper Dependence on God

When everything else is stripped away, the only thing left to stand on is Him. And that's exactly where God wants us.

Not leaning on comfort.
Not propped up by applause.
Not sustained by circumstances.
But dependent. Fully. Desperately. Daily.

This is where intimacy is born—not in the spotlight, but in the shadows. In the quiet. In the pain. In the waiting. In the moments when your strength fails, and all that's left is His strength holding you up.

> *"For the mountains may depart and the hills be removed,*
> *but my steadfast love shall not depart from you,*
> *and my covenant of peace shall not be removed,"*
> *says the Lord, who has compassion on you.."*
> —Isaiah 54:10 (ESV)

You may walk out of the furnace with scars. You may come out with stories that still sting. But you'll also come out with fire in your bones, steel in your spirit, and a faith that's not for sale. Because once you've stood in the fire with God, you don't fear the flames anymore.

Forged for the Fire

The furnace isn't where you break down. It's where you're built. God doesn't waste fire; He uses it:

- To strip away what's superficial.
- To expose what's eternal.
- To forge in you a strength that this shaking world cannot crush.

Just as iron must pass through fire to become steel—your faith is being forged. Not melted down, but hammered into resilience. The heat, the pressure, the pounding—none of it is random. It's refining your structure. Strengthening your soul. Shaping your spirit.

The world may look at you and only see scars. But Heaven sees a weapon in the hand of God—tempered by trial, unwavering in truth.

Romans 8:29 says that we are being "conformed to the image of His Son."

That's not surface-level change. That's deep forging. And it doesn't happen in comfort; it happens in the crucible.

So if you're in the fire right now…

Don't fear it. Don't curse it.
Stand in it. Lean into it.
Because God isn't trying to destroy you—
He's preparing to deploy you.
You're being forged for the fight.
Strengthened for the shaking.
Refined for the mission.
When you emerge from this furnace, you won't just survive it—
You'll shine.

REMNANT RISING

3

FOUNDATIONS THAT ENDURE

We've all seen what happens when the shaking comes;
Some people panic.
Some compromise.
Some collapse.
And then there are those who stand.
Not because they're stronger than everyone else, but because they're anchored to something deeper. Something immovable. *Someone* immovable.

> *"I have set the Lord always before me; because He is at my right hand, I shall not be shaken."* —Psalm 16:8

Let's be clear—standing unshaken doesn't mean untouched. It doesn't mean you won't feel the tremors of loss, fear, betrayal, pressure, or pain. It means when the winds blow and the waves crash, your life is not built on shifting sand.

It's built on the Rock.

We're not promised an easy life. We're promised a firm foundation. Jesus didn't say the storm *might* come—He said it *will*.

In Matthew 7, He tells of two men who each built a house. One on the rock. One on the sand. The same storm hit both. Only one house stood. The wise hear the words of the Master and put them into practice. The foolish hear and do nothing. The storm doesn't reveal who we think we are—it reveals what we're actually built on.

So How Do We Stand?

How do we live with conviction when the world demands compromise?
How do we stay steady when culture calls us intolerant, foolish, or extreme?
How do we stay rooted when emotions run high, headlines get worse, and spiritual warfare hits our home?

We plant our feet.
We anchor our souls.
We lock eyes with Jesus, and we refuse to move.

Not out of stubbornness—but out of faith. Because standing isn't a passive posture: it's a warrior stance. And in this chapter, we're going to explore how to take it and how to keep it.

Foundations vs. Facades

I recently heard this joke:

A lawyer had just finished parking in front of the courthouse. As he stepped out of his BMW, a speeding car flew by and ripped the door clean off. The lawyer started jumping up and down, swearing at his misfortune.
A police officer who witnessed the whole thing came running over, shaking his head. "You lawyers make me sick! You're so materialistic. You're so concerned about your precious BMW that you didn't even notice your left arm is missing!"
The lawyer looked down at his bloody stump and screamed, "Oh no! My Rolex!"

Now… it's just a joke. But isn't there a sting of truth in it? Do you ever wonder if society has misplaced its values? We're a culture obsessed with the external. The image. The performance. The brand. We fuss over how things look—even while they're falling apart underneath.

Too many Christians know how to appear "put together"—but not how to be unshakable.. They've built a beautiful spiritual façade on a foundation of sand. And then the storm hits and it all comes crashing down around them.

Jesus didn't say, "The foolish man didn't love God." He said the foolish man didn't build well. The difference wasn't his passion—it was his foundation. And foundations aren't tested in fair weather—they're tested in storms. Faithfulness is key. It holds us steady when the winds rise.

When the Church Becomes a Stage

Let's be honest. In many corners of the modern church, we've gotten really good at producing the image of faith—without always building the substance of it. We know how to clap at the right moments. We know how to post the perfect Scripture meme. We know how to smile through the service, lift our hands in the worship music, shout "Amen!" during the message, only to go home exhausted, anxious, and unchanged.

Why? Because image is easier than intimacy. Performance is easier than presence. A façade is easier to build than a foundation. We have churches full of people who look strong on Sunday, but crumble on Monday. When the pandemic hit, when the world began to shake, when real pressure came—many believers realized their roots didn't go as deep as they thought. Some fell away entirely. Others numbed out. Others tried to push through but found themselves drifting in a spiritual fog.

> *You don't build a foundation during the flood. You build it in the quiet before the storm.*

The hard truth? Shallow teaching builds shallow faith. Entertainment-driven Christianity doesn't prepare you for a furnace, and motivational soundbites won't help you when the storm is howling.

God never called His people to be pretty; He called us to be planted.

Jesus taught about two houses—both of which looked the same from the outside. They were likely similar in appearance, structure, and maybe even cost. But when the storm hit, only one stood.

Why? Because it was built on the rock.

The fact is, you can't see a foundation until it's tested.

Your devotional life? That's your foundation.

Your prayer life? Foundation.

Your obedience in private? Foundation.

Your love for the Word, your willingness to forgive, your refusal to compromise when no one is watching—that's the real structure beneath the surface.

And when everything else shakes, that's what will keep you standing.

The remnant doesn't need to be flashy; it needs to be fortified.

We don't need a platform. We need a plumb line. The days of playing church are over. It's time to dig deep.

Spiritual Disciplines that Anchor You

We don't become unshakable by accident. We become unshakable by training for the trial before it arrives. If you wait until the shaking to build your foundation, you're already behind. That's why spiritual disciplines aren't just "good Christian habits"—they are your survival gear. Here are four that anchor the remnant:

1. **Prayer: The Place Where Power is Birthed**

   Prayer isn't a polite ritual—it's a soul-level cry that moves heaven. Think of Hannah, weeping bitterly in the temple, crying out to God for a child. Her prayer was so raw, so passionate, that Eli the priest thought she was intoxicated. But God heard her, and Samuel—the prophet who would anoint kings—was born from that kind of prayer.

   Prayer isn't about eloquence. It's about persistence, intensity, and intimacy. When you pray like your life depends on it, things shift.

2. **The Word of God: Your Sword and Shield**

   In the wilderness, Jesus didn't argue with Satan—He quoted Scripture. "It is written..." was His weapon of choice. If the Son of God relied on memorized Scripture to battle the enemy, how much more do we need to know the Word? This isn't optional. This is survival.

   The Word is alive. It will sustain you in famine, correct you in pride, comfort you in sorrow, and rebuke every lie from the pit of hell. The remnant must not merely read the Word—we must live it, speak it, and wield it.

3. **Obedience: Trust in Action**

   Obedience doesn't always make sense—but it always makes a difference.

   Abraham left everything familiar just because God said "Go."

   Joshua led his army to march silently around a fortified city—no logic, no battle plan, just radical trust.

   Ruth, the Moabite, obeyed Naomi's unusual instructions and laid herself at Boaz's feet—a quiet, obedient act that honored her mother-in-law, opened the door for her redemption, and placed her in the lineage of Jesus—the long-awaited Messiah.

And of course, **Jesus** Himself—the perfect picture of obedience—said, "I do nothing except what I see the Father doing."

Obedience isn't just agreement. It's alignment. When the world shakes, obedience becomes your anchor of trust. It keeps you tethered to the heart of God, even when the path doesn't make sense.

4. **Authentic Community: Strength in the Fold**

   You weren't meant to stand alone. Isolation makes you vulnerable. But real, Spirit-filled fellowship sharpens, encourages, and covers you when you're under fire. The remnant was never meant to be a remnant of one.

   In Acts 2:42, we see the early church devoted to one another—breaking bread, praying together, sharing resources, and walking in supernatural unity. That kind of fellowship didn't just feel good—it carried power.

Throughout the Bible, we see the strength of community:

- ❖ **Israel**, called and formed as a nation of priests with a corporate identity and mission.
- ❖ **David**, surrounded by a loyal band of mighty men who stood with him through war, wilderness, and betrayal.
- ❖ **Paul**, writing in 1 Corinthians 12:25–27 about the Body of Christ: *"If one member suffers, all suffer together; if one is honored, all rejoice together."*

You were never intended to fight alone. The remnant thrives in covenant connection, not shallow fellowship. You need people who will pray you through the fire, call you out when you drift, and lift you up when the battle gets heavy.

This is Your Time to Dig Deep

The shaking isn't over—and more is coming. But here's the good news: God has already given you everything you need to stand. *Not just* to survive, but to withstand. *Not just* to endure, but to advance. But you must decide what kind of foundation you're going to build on.

Not tomorrow. Not when life slows down. Not when things feel easier; Now.
Now is the time to anchor your life in prayer that goes deeper than words.
Now is the time to feast on the Word of God until it lives in your bones.
Now is the time to obey when it's uncomfortable, when it's unclear, when it costs you.
Now is the time to press into community—to be known, to be sharpened, to be carried when you're weak, and to carry others who need your strength.
This is how the remnant rises.
Not with hype, but with holiness.
Not with noise, but with depth.
Not with a platform, but with a foundation.
Dig deep. Stand firm. Stay anchored. Because the days ahead will require everything you've got… and everything He is.

"The wise man built his house upon the rock…" —Matthew 7:24
Take this to heart. Carry it into battle.

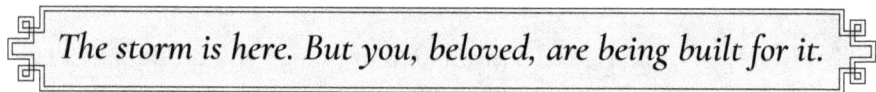

The storm is here. But you, beloved, are being built for it.

Closing Charge: Commissioned to Build Deep

You cannot fake a foundation.
You either build deep—or you collapse when the storm comes.
The time to build is now.

- Dig into prayer.
- Saturate yourself in the Word.
- Obey even when it stretches you.
- Find a community that sharpens and strengthens you.

When the shaking intensifies—and believe me, it will—only what is anchored will endure.

4

Refined for Battle, Ready for Purpose

There's a reason God is refining the remnant. It's not just to make you stronger. It's to make you ready. We're not being purified for comfort—we're being prepared for combat. And not just any kind of combat: spiritual, emotional, cultural, and deeply personal. We are not living in peacetime. This is an hour of shaking, sifting, and spiritual warfare, and if you're part of the remnant, you've probably felt it already.

But hear me clearly: the pressure doesn't mean you're failing—it means you're on assignment.

The Remnant Feels the Pressure First

If you've been feeling tired, misunderstood, or even spiritually targeted, it's not because you're weak—it's because you're on the front lines. The remnant is always the first to feel the intensity of the battle.

You may experience:

- **Isolation:** feeling like few people around you see what you see.
- **Rejection:** being misunderstood or pushed aside by friends, family, even the church.

- **Fatigue:** fighting spiritual battles no one else seems to notice.
- **Inner conflict:** knowing you're called to speak, to take a stand, to *do* something, but fearing backlash or failure.

You're not "losing it"—and you're not dismissed. You're being forged and focused—because the remnant doesn't blend in. The remnant goes before.

I know what it feels like to be rejected—not by the world, but by the very people you thought would recognize and affirm your calling.

Years ago, after leaving Mormonism and discovering the richness of biblical Christianity, I was on fire to grow, learn, and serve. I applied to a Baptist seminary, believing this could be the next step in preparing for ministry.

But my application was rejected. The reason? I had been divorced. No room for nuance. No inquiry into my walk with the Lord or the healing He had done in my life. Just a firm, silent door—slammed shut. Not based on my gifting. Not based on my theology. Based on my past.

And that's when a quiet lie crept in and started building a false theology in my soul: *"You blew it. You stained God's name. You can still be kind and helpful, but your leadership days are over. You're damaged goods."*

I didn't question it right away. I accepted it. It stung deeper than I expected. It wasn't just a closed door—it felt like a verdict: You are disqualified. You are tainted. You are not fit to serve the Lord. I carried it like a spiritual sentence, choosing invisibility over influence, service over calling, support over speaking.

But the holy unrest inside me refused to quiet. That fire—that same unshakable sense of calling I'd felt even as a child—kept rising. The Holy Spirit began whispering and broke through the rubble of rejection with a different narrative that spoke truth and affirmation:

"Your worth is not determined by man's interpretation of Scripture.

Your calling is not canceled by your story.

And I don't 'just tolerate' broken vessels—I choose them."

Rejection by man doesn't revoke your assignment from God. In fact, sometimes it confirms it—because God often raises up those the religious system would never choose.

You Were Born for This

It's easy to think, "Someone else is better equipped." But God didn't call someone else. He called *you*.

Your voice.

Your story.

Your scars.
Your sensitivity.
Your discernment.
Your fire.
You are not here by accident. You were born into this generation because this is your time.

> *"Who knows but that you have come to the Kingdom for such a time as this?"* —Esther 4:14

God doesn't waste seasons of pain, loss, or transition. He uses them to sharpen your awareness, deepen your faith, and build a kind of boldness that doesn't make headlines—but *terrifies hell*.

BROKENNESS DOESN'T DISQUALIFY—IT PREPARES

Throughout Scripture, it's the wounded, the flawed, the misunderstood, and the unlikely who are chosen by God to carry out some of the most powerful Kingdom assignments.

- Moses had a stutter and a temper.
- David committed adultery and murder, yet was called "a man after God's own heart."
- Rahab was a prostitute, but played a pivotal role in the lineage of Christ.
- Peter denied Jesus—three times. And yet Jesus still said, "Feed My sheep."
- Paul once persecuted Christians, yet became one of the greatest apostles in history.

If you think your story disqualifies you, you haven't read the stories God loves to write. He delights in using cracked jars because His glory shines all the brighter through the broken places.

You don't need to hide your scars, edit your testimony, or pretend to be whole.

> *God shines brightest through vessels that have been shattered and surrendered.*

The Remnant Is Being Readied for Purpose

The refining wasn't random. The wilderness wasn't wasted. The rejection wasn't the end of your story—it was the beginning of your commissioning.

So now what?

What does it look like for the remnant to move from being forged to being deployed? It begins with one powerful, Spirit-filled word: discernment.

How the Remnant Discerns Its Role

The remnant doesn't run ahead blindly. We listen. We wait. We watch for movement. You don't need to manufacture a ministry or invent a mission. You need to recognize the assignment God is already placing in front of you.

Ask yourself:

What burdens won't let me go?

Who are the people I naturally weep for?

What truth burns in my bones?

Where do I keep sensing the Spirit nudge me, even when it scares me?

Your calling may not be grand or public—it might be deeply personal and profoundly impactful. You might be called to raise warriors. To disciple one. To write, teach, speak, intercede, build, serve, plant, mentor, heal. But whatever it is, it matters.

The remnant isn't about status. It's about surrendered strategy. You weren't just called to be refined. You were called to be released!

> *"The Spirit of the Lord is upon me, because He has anointed me to preach good news to the poor... to proclaim liberty to the captives... to declare the year of the Lord's favor."* —Luke 4:18–19

Trust the Timing, Trust the Terrain

The weight of calling can feel heavy, especially when you're still waiting for clarity, open doors, or confirmation. But friend, God is not just writing your story—He's directing its release.

He sees what you don't. He knows who you're becoming. And He is far more invested in your fruitfulness than your platform. You may feel hidden. You may feel slow to launch. You may wonder why others are running ahead while you're still walking. But let me tell you something: Jesus spent 30 years in preparation for a 3-year ministry that would change the world.

Preparation isn't a punishment—it's a prophetic setup. If you try to force the timing, you may get ahead of the grace. If you try to expand the reach on your own, you may outgrow your roots.

The assignment God has for you will be revealed at the right time, to the right people, in the right way. Your job is not to control the outcome, but to stay ready.

Whether He places you before thousands or entrusts you with a few…

Whether He calls you to sow in secret or speak on a stage…

Whether your assignment seems small or significant…

It is sacred.

You were forged for this.

Appointed for this.

Sent into this generation on purpose.

So stand ready! Your assignment may be smaller than you expected, or greater than you dreamed. But it will be exactly what the Kingdom needs.

Stay low. Stay yielded. Stay watchful. The remnant doesn't chase impact—we carry presence. And when the time comes to rise, you'll be ready.

Closing Charge: Commissioned to Stand

You are on assignment.

Your faith is being deepened.

Let God shine through the cracks in your armor.

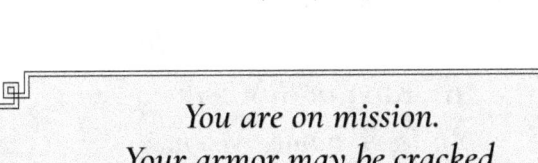

You are on mission.
Your armor may be cracked,
but your calling is not canceled.

Closing Prayer

Father God,
You are the Rock that cannot be moved.
You are the Anchor that holds
when everything else gives way.

Today, I commit to stand.
Strengthen my legs when they tremble.
Steady my hands when they shake.
Fortify my heart when fear whispers.

Let me be a watchman, a warrior, a witness—
unashamed and unafraid.
Let my life echo the faithfulness
of those who came before me.
Let me be counted worthy
to stand in this hour.
In Jesus' name, Amen.

5

COURAGE IN THE FACE OF CHAOS

There is a courage that doesn't come from ourselves. It's not about bravado or ego-fueled defiance. It's not the temporary adrenaline of the moment. It's a courage birthed in the fire of faith—a resilience that grows when everything around us shakes.

In these last days, the remnant will need more than opinions and observations. We will need courage. Real courage.

The kind that says, "Even if I lose everything, I will not bow."
The kind that says, "Even if I stand alone, I will stand."
The kind that says, "Even if my voice trembles, I will still speak truth."

THE REALITY OF THE BATTLE

Isaiah 54:17 reminds us:

No weapon that is formed against you will succeed;
And every tongue that accuses you in judgment you will condemn.
This is the heritage of the servants of the Lord,
And their vindication is from Me," declares the Lord.

Notice that it doesn't say weapons won't be formed. They will be. It doesn't say accusations won't come. They *will* come. But it promises that the weapons and accusations will not prosper against those who are anchored in the Lord. We are entering a time when bold faith will be costly, when standing for biblical truth will be seen as extremism, and when speaking the name of Jesus without compromise may invite hatred—or worse. We must settle in our hearts now that courage isn't optional for the remnant. It's part of our spiritual DNA.

Real Stories of Courage

Esther

She wasn't raised in a palace. She didn't grow up dreaming of being royalty. She was a Jewish orphan living in exile under Persian rule. And yet, by God's design, she was brought into the king's court and chosen as queen.

When an evil plot was uncovered to exterminate the Jews, Esther was faced with a decision that could cost her life: approach the king uninvited, or stay silent and hope someone else would intervene.

In that time, no one could enter the king's presence without being summoned. To do so could mean death—unless the king extended his golden scepter in mercy. Esther didn't know what would happen. She didn't know if she would live or die. But she knew she had come to that position for a purpose. So she fasted. She prayed. And she went.

"If I perish, I perish," she said. But she would not remain silent.

That's what courage looks like—it's not being unafraid. It's moving forward despite the fear.

Elisha

He wasn't surrounded by friends. He wasn't backed by an army. He was a prophet of God, trapped in a city now encircled by enemy forces. Horses. Chariots. Soldiers. A great army sent to capture just one man.

At dawn, his servant went outside and saw the terrifying sight. They were everywhere. There was no way out.

"Alas, my master!" he cried. "What shall we do?"

But Elisha didn't panic. He didn't crumble. He spoke a truth that didn't match what human eyes could see.

"Do not be afraid," he said. "For those who are with us are more than those who are with them."

Then he prayed a simple prayer:

"O Lord, open his eyes that he may see."

In an instant, the servant's fear gave way to awe. The hills around the city were ablaze with chariots of fire—heaven's army, vast and mighty, standing guard.

The battle was never about numbers. It was about who stood with them.

That's what courage looks like—it's not trusting what your eyes see. It's trusting the One who sees it all.

Peter and the apostles

They were preaching Jesus with boldness and power, healing the sick, turning hearts to truth. The religious leaders were furious—threatened by the crowds and enraged by the name of Jesus being proclaimed. So they had the men arrested. Put them in prison. Tried to stop the move of God with metal bars and angry threats.

But God sent an angel—not to hide them, not to comfort them in chains, but to rescue them with a charge:

"Go, stand and speak to the people in the temple the whole message of this Life." (Acts 5:20)

And that's exactly what they did. Even knowing it might mean further imprisonment. Even knowing it might lead to death.

They stood.

They spoke.

They obeyed.

And though they were flogged and humiliated, they didn't retreat—they rejoiced and persevered.

"They went on their way... rejoicing that they had been considered worthy to suffer shame for His name. And every day... they kept right on teaching and preaching Jesus as the Christ." (Acts 5:41–42)

William Tyndale

He wasn't trying to start a war. He wasn't seeking fame. He simply believed that every man, woman, and child should be able to read the Word of God in their own language.

But in his day, the Bible was locked away in Latin—a language most common people couldn't understand. The Church guarded it fiercely. To translate Scripture into English was forbidden and considered a crime against both crown and pope.

Tyndale knew the risks. He knew what it could cost him. But he also knew the truth was worth fighting for. He fled England. He lived in exile. And still, he worked. He translated. He smuggled English Bibles back across the Channel, hidden in barrels and sacks of grain. His work sparked a movement that could not be stopped.

Eventually, he was betrayed. Captured. Condemned. Tyndale's final words before his execution were a prayer: "Lord, open the King of England's eyes."

He died for the Word of God—but he did not die in vain.

Within a few years, English Bibles were being printed by royal decree, just as he had prayed.

That's what courage looks like—it's not surviving at all costs. It's standing for the truth, no matter the cost. These are the kinds of men and women God uses to change history.

Not the fearless, but the faithful.

Not the loudest, but the obedient.

The Courage to Stand in Small Places

Courage isn't always standing before kings or being led to execution.

Sometimes it's standing firm in the small, hidden places—where no one but God sees.

Sometimes courage looks like a young man who refuses to cheat when everyone else in his class is passing around the answers.

> *Courage isn't in knowing how things will turn out— it's in trusting God with the outcome and showing up anyway.*

Sometimes courage looks like a single mom who keeps praying and providing, even when she feels invisible and exhausted.

Sometimes courage looks like a factory worker who won't lie to cover up a mistake, even when it could cost him his job.

Sometimes courage looks like a teenager who walks away from a group of friends making fun of someone weaker.

Sometimes courage looks like an ordinary homeschool mom standing up at a county meeting, trembling with nerves and tearfully defending the right of parents to educate their children.

Years ago, when I was homeschooling my children in Las Vegas, the county was considering new restrictions that could have made it harder for families like mine. I didn't want to go. I didn't feel brave. I wasn't a polished speaker or a political activist—I was just a mom who cared deeply about her calling.

But something inside whispered, "Why not you?"
So I went. And I stood. And with a shaking voice and tear-filled eyes, I spoke.
I didn't have influence. I didn't have connections. But I had conviction.
And that day, the decision turned in favor of homeschoolers.

I believe my voice made a difference—not because I was strong, but because God gave me courage when I needed it most.

Courage doesn't always make headlines—but it always matters.

Your Courage Will Cost You

We need to be honest about this part, too. Courage will cost you your comfort. Your popularity. Your safe, predictable, undisturbed life. It might cost you relationships. Opportunities. Open doors. Invitations. Even income. But what you gain is worth infinitely more:

Peace that can't be shaken.
Joy that doesn't make sense.
Fellowship with the suffering Savior.
And the unshakable knowledge that you are walking in obedience—even if you walk alone.

Courage will cost you—but it will also shape you.
And the good news is, courage isn't reserved for the special few.
It's something you can grow.
It's something you can cultivate—step by step, choice by choice, as you trust God in the hard places.

*Courage is not something you either have or don't have;
it's something you practice.*

Practical Ways to Cultivate Courage

Here are ways to build and strengthen courage:

> **Pray Bold Prayers:** Ask God to make you bold, not safe. Ask Him to give you the heart of a lion clothed in the humility of a lamb.

> **Strengthen Your Foundations:** Spend time daily in the Word, remembering who God is and who you are in Him. Faith feeds courage.

- ➤ **Take Small Risks Daily:** Courage grows when exercised. Speak truth in small ways. Step into obedience. Little yeses prepare you for bigger ones.
- ➤ **Refuse to Bow to Fear:** Fear is a spirit. Rebuke it. Name it. Replace it with truth.
- ➤ **Remember Who Fights for You:** You are not standing alone. The Captain of the Hosts of Heaven stands with you.

Joy as a Weapon

Another surprising key to courage is joy.
Nehemiah 8:10 declares:
"Do not grieve, for the joy of the Lord is your strength."
Joy is not passive. It's active warfare. When we choose to rejoice—even in trial—we rob the enemy of his weapons against us.
Joy declares:
"You can't steal my hope."
"You can't silence my song."
"You can't define my destiny."
Joy says God's promises are bigger than my pain. And joy fuels courage in ways that fear never can.

Closing Charge: Rise, Speak, Stand

The world is trembling.
Truth is falling in the streets.
The love of many is growing cold.
Now is not the time for silent saints or hidden lights.
The remnant must be the ones who rise. Who speak. Who stand.
Even if our voices shake.
Even if our knees tremble.
Even if the crowds turn against us.
We stand because Christ stood for us.
We speak because we carry the only message that can save.
We rise because darkness is no match for the light of God in us.

Commissioning Prayer

Father, clothe us with courage from heaven.
Teach us to stand when others sit down.
Teach us to speak when others stay silent.

Fill us with boldness fueled not by anger, but by love.
Let the roar of the Lion of Judah echo in our spirits.
Make us warriors who fight on our knees
and shine with Your glory.

We refuse to bow to fear.
We refuse to retreat in shame.
We will stand firm, speak truth, and shine with joy.
In Jesus' name, Amen.

> *Faithful courage is not reckless—*
> *it's rooted in the trust that*
> *God holds the outcome.*

Remnant Rising

6

Eyes to See in the Age of AI

We are living in a time of unprecedented advancement. What once took hours now takes seconds. What was once unreachable now fits in the palm of our hand. In many ways, technology—especially artificial intelligence—has become a powerful tool of connection, creation, and even compassion.

AI has helped diagnose rare diseases and develop life-saving treatments. People with disabilities have been given new ways to communicate, to write, to work, and to thrive. It's been used to translate Bibles into unreached languages. Ministries have deployed chatbots to respond instantly to seekers in closed nations where gospel access is limited.

During times of isolation, technology became the thread that kept people connected: Livestreamed church services, virtual Bible studies, prayer gatherings over Zoom or similar video conferencing programs.

Even platforms like ChatGPT have been used to help believers study Scripture, write devotionals, prepare sermons, and organize ministry ideas. Technology has opened doors that once seemed impossible.

In the right hands, it is a blessing.

A tool.

A gift.

But every gift carries a responsibility.

And every tool can become a weapon in the wrong hands.

The "What Ifs" That Demand Discernment

What if the same AI that helps write devotionals is later stripped of access to the Bible?

What if algorithms are trained only on ideas that align with secular ideologies—rewriting history, removing virtue, and replacing truth with carefully crafted narratives?

What happens when our books are banned, our voices silenced, and the digital cloud no longer carries the wisdom of the ages—but carries only the propaganda of the hour?

It might sound dystopian, but the trajectory is already in motion. We've seen the subtle (and not so subtle) erosion of free speech. The quiet suppression of biblical truth in public forums. The redefinition of long-held values.

And what if it goes even further? What if humans begin to merge with machines—through brain-AI interfaces like Neuralink?

What if people no longer seek truth but simply download consensus? When everyone thinks the same—not because they're united in the Spirit, but because they're connected to the same artificial source?

These are not science fiction fantasies. They're warnings worth heeding. Because once truth is no longer welcomed in the system, those who carry it must be ready to stand apart from the system.

As in the Days of Noah

In **Genesis 6:5**, we read of a time when the earth was saturated with evil.

"Every intention of the thoughts of his heart was only evil continually."

It was a generation marked by violence, corruption, and a total abandonment of righteousness. That wasn't just a cultural problem; it was a spiritual tipping point. And God responded not with reform—but with a flood.

Jesus warned that the last days would mirror the days of Noah. A time when people would be distracted, indulgent, and spiritually blind to the judgment approaching. Evil wouldn't be isolated—it would be normalized. Celebrated. Embedded into every system.

Daniel foresaw a time when knowledge would increase and people would run to and fro; a picture of a fast-paced, information-saturated world that nevertheless grows cold and confused.

Revelation paints an even more dramatic scene:

A beast system.

Global control.

False worship.

People deceived by signs and wonders—not unlike the illusions we see emerging today through deepfakes, virtual realities, and persuasive lies dressed in digital light.

The Rise of Deepfakes—Digital and Demonic

We're entering an age where you can no longer trust your eyes or ears. Deepfakes—AI-generated videos and voices—are growing so advanced that it's nearly impossible to tell what's real and what's fabricated.

A world leader can be made to "declare war" without ever opening their mouth. A pastor's voice can be cloned to preach heresy. A loved one can call you for help—but it's not them. It's a synthetic fraud. These aren't just pranks; they're tools of confusion, blackmail, manipulation, psychological warfare.

Used by the wrong hands, with nefarious motives, deepfakes can rewrite reality. They can spark fear, spread lies, incite violence, or turn the masses against a person who's done nothing wrong. The more we rely on screens and devices for truth, the more susceptible we are to these illusions.

> *Jacob wore goat hair to mimic Esau. Satan masquerades as an angel of light. The Antichrist will declare himself God. Deepfakes aren't new—they're just digital versions of ancient deceptions.*

And yet—this is nothing new. The devil has been crafting deepfakes since the Garden. Jacob disguised himself as Esau, covering his arms in goat hair and fooling his father's senses. It was a literal deepfake—designed to deceive his father and steal a blessing.

Paul warned of false apostles who disguised themselves as messengers of righteousness; *"For Satan himself transforms himself into an angel of light."* (2 Corinthians 11:14). Not just darkness pretending to be light—but the perfect counterfeit of holiness.

The Antichrist, Scripture says, will come with signs and lying wonders—deceiving even the elect, if that were possible. He will sit in the temple and declare himself to be God. Not just a political leader. A spiritual deepfake pretending to be divine.

And as we approach the end of the age, more deception is coming. Some speculate about Project Blue Beam, a proposed government project that could simulate false signs in the sky—holograms, voices, "miraculous" appearances—engineered to usher in a global deception.

Others point to the sudden normalization of the alien narrative, wondering if demonic or fallen angelic beings might one day masquerade as "extraterrestrial visitors." Bringing false peace. False unity. A false gospel from "the stars."

The Bible tells us plainly: *Satan is not creative—he's a counterfeit artist.*

He twists what God made. He imitates the miraculous. He creates spectacles to distract from truth. And as technology advances, his tools of deception grow sharper. That's why the remnant must walk not by sight. Not by sound. Not by emotion. But by the Spirit of truth. Because when the fake becomes indistinguishable from the real, only those who know the voice of the Shepherd will recognize the difference.

The Remnant Response

More than ever, we need people who carry the Word of God in their hearts, not just on their screens. People who can discern truth when the internet cannot. People who are grounded—not in algorithms, but in the anointing of the Holy Spirit. The remnant must be:

Carriers of truth in a time of deception.

Bearers of light in a world growing dim.

Messengers of hope in a generation overwhelmed by fear.

We must raise up Daniels—those who can interpret the signs of the time without compromising their integrity.

We must equip Esthers—those who are willing to speak, even if it costs them their comfort, their platform, or even their lives.

We must train watchmen—those who are awake while others sleep, standing on the wall and warning with love, not panic.

This is not the time to retreat from technology. It's the time to redeem it. We must use the tools available while remaining untangled from the systems of the world. Me must plant the Word deep in our hearts while we still can—and teach others to do the same.

Technology can simulate almost anything.
Discernment shows what's real.

I used to think the story of redemption began and ended with Adam and Eve. But then I encountered the work of Dr. Michael Heiser—and it was like someone pulled back the veil to reveal things I had not considered.

Suddenly I saw a war in the heavens, divine rebellions, and territorial claims that stretched across Scripture. Jesus didn't just come to redeem mankind. He came to disarm the powers and principalities, to reclaim what was forfeited, and to establish God's Kingdom on Earth. As Heiser wrote in *The Unseen Realm*: *"The kingdom of God is not about going to heaven; it's about bringing God's rule to earth."*

That one sentence reframed everything for me. I no longer see myself as just a saved soul. I see myself as a commissioned agent of the King. That's what it means to be part of the remnant.

Momentum demands movement.
If the Spirit is prompting you, act.

As the shadows deepen and deception grows bolder, the remnant must do more than see—we must stand. Clarity is only the beginning. What good is discernment without the courage to act on it? In a world gripped by confusion, compromise, and chaos, God is looking for those who won't flinch, won't flee, and won't fold under pressure. Because the days ahead won't just test what we believe—they will test what we're willing to risk for the truth.

AI is a tool. Discernment is a weapon.

CLOSING CHARGE: ANCHORED AND ABLAZE

The future may bring more confusion.
More deception.
More technological marvels that blur the line between real and false.
But the Spirit of God has not changed. The Word of God still stands.
And the call to the remnant is clearer than ever:
Stay anchored. Stay alert. Stay ablaze.

Don't put your trust in tools—put it in Truth.
Don't fear the systems of men—fear the Lord.
Don't follow the crowd—follow the cloud of His presence.
Because in a world that may soon be run by machines…
Only the Spirit-filled will have the wisdom to lead.

✧ ✧ ✧

When the Sun Roars:
A Modern-Day Carrington?

In 1859, a massive solar storm—now known as the Carrington Event—slammed into Earth's magnetic field and lit up the skies around the globe. Telegraph machines sparked. Auroras danced as far south as the Caribbean. Technology at the time was primitive, but even so, the storm left its mark.

Now imagine something like that hitting today. Power grids would fail. Satellites could be damaged or destroyed. GPS, internet, and communication systems could go dark. No ATMs. No fuel. No refrigeration. In some places, it could take months to recover.

Scientists say it's not just possible—it's inevitable. A similar near-miss happened in 2012, and NASA estimates there's roughly a 12% chance per decade of another Carrington-level event. During periods of solar maximum—like the one we are currently entering—solar flares and magnetic storms intensify.

And yet, as serious as that sounds, the remnant does not panic. We do not fear the shaking. We were born for it.

We don't bank our peace on working power grids—we bank it on the power of God. We don't look to satellites for direction—we listen for the Shepherd's voice. And we don't hide from the storm—we stand firm in the One who calms it.

Let the sun roar if it must.
The Light of the World will never go out.

✦ ✦ ✦

What Shape Is the Earth— And Does It Matter?

Some believe the Earth is flat—or shaped like an upside-down frisbee, with Antarctica as its icy outer edge. The theory sounds compelling to those who distrust mainstream science or see biblical references to the "four corners of the Earth" as literal descriptions.

But while healthy skepticism is wise, not all alternative views are rooted in truth. From satellite photos and time zones to gravity and eclipsess—overwhelming evidence confirms Earth is a sphere.

Scripture was never meant to be a science textbook. It's a revelation of God, not a schematic of creation. And while it's good to ask questions, we must be careful not to chase distractions that pull us away from the true battlefield.

The shape of the Earth may be debated.
But the mission of the remnant is not.

✦ ✦ ✦

7

THE RISING TIDE OF DECEPTION

While we've been learning to navigate the digital deception—deepfakes, AI manipulation, and the ever-expanding technological web—there's an even deeper one rising beneath it all. One that's older than the internet, older than nations, older than history itself.

You see, the enemy's playbook isn't limited to technology—it's ancient. It's spiritual. It's the same dark agenda that has been at work since the garden, and it's resurfacing now with greater intensity than ever before.

If we think artificial intelligence is the only thing we need to watch for, we'll miss the larger picture. The strong delusion of the last days is multi-layered—and it's about more than machines. It's about giants, ancient gods, spiritual infiltration, and the return of dark powers once thought defeated.

Let's go there. Let's uncover what's really rising—and how the remnant can stand unshaken in the midst of it all. If you're like me, you're probably asking:

How do we live when we know what's coming, but still have to go about daily life?

How do we balance the everyday—bills to pay, mouths to feed, kids to raise, groceries to buy—with the looming reality that the world is unraveling?

I think back to 2019, before what some have called the "scamdemic" flipped everything upside down. It's easy to be sarcastic about it, given how the crisis was used to exert control over the global population—but the virus itself was real.

The problem wasn't so much the illness—it was how fear and manipulation were weaponized to reshape the world.

Prior to that event, I was doing all kinds of things—learning Spanish, studying for my ham radio license, making digital art for Etsy. And then it felt like the whole world shifted. The global agenda was moving fast, and I thought:

This is it. The proverbial manure is about to hit the fan. What's the point in learning Spanish or creating art when the world as we know it is coming to an end?

So I stopped. I dropped my hobbies, my creativity, even my long-term goals. But here we are—five years later. The world is still spinning. Yes, it's darker, and yes, the signs are intensifying, but the End hasn't come yet. And I look back and think: By now I could have been fluent in Spanish, a licensed ham operator, and running a thriving Etsy shop.

The question remains: How do we live and prepare at the same time?

Do we send our kids to college, encourage them to get married, start a family, build a life? Or do we tell them to hunker down and wait for "The End?"

Do we focus on paying off debt, storing six months of food, learning survival skills, building an off-grid shelter… or do we just trust God to handle it all?

I know the "spiritual" answer is: *Be led by the Spirit*. And that's true. But it's also a weight on many people's minds. It's a tension we feel every day—how do we stay watchful without living in fear? How do we prepare without falling into paralysis or panic?

How do we, as the remnant, rise above dread and indecision—and actually bring the Kingdom to earth, while we're still living in a broken world?

That's the question we need to keep at the front of our hearts as we walk through the rest of this chapter. Because yes, deception is coming. Giants, ancient spirits, aliens—it's all coming. But so is God's plan for His remnant.

As in the Days of Noah… and Lot

Jesus gave us a roadmap. He told us exactly what the last days would look like:

"As it was in the days of Noah, so it will be at the coming of the Son of Man." (Matthew 24:37)

"Likewise, just as it was in the days of Lot… so it will be on the day when the Son of Man is revealed." (Luke 17:28–30)

That wasn't a random comparison. It was a warning—because the days of Noah and Lot were marked by specific patterns we need to recognize.

In Noah's time, the world was filled with violence, lawlessness, and something far more sinister: the corruption of the human genome. Genesis 6 tells us that the sons of God (Benei ha-Elohim) took human women as wives and had children with them—resulting in the Nephilim, a hybrid race that defiled God's design. It was an age of genetic rebellion, of mixing what God had separated. And it wasn't just about giant bodies—it was about giant wickedness.

In Lot's day, it was perversion, lawlessness, and a total breakdown of moral order. The people of Sodom and Gomorrah were consumed with lust, violence, and self-gratification, to the point where they demanded to assault angelic visitors. And yet, society saw nothing wrong with it. They had been fully desensitized.

Jesus was warning us: these patterns will repeat in the last days.

And they are.

Today we see gender confusion, transhumanism, gene editing, and AI-driven biological manipulation—new faces of an old rebellion. We see the rise of lawlessness, the normalization of perversion, and the celebration of sin. We see spirits of violence unleashed in the streets and in homes. We see it in the redefinition of family, the destruction of innocence, and the open defiance of God's design.

The "days of Noah" are not just a historical reference—they're a prophetic blueprint for the future.

There's even a fringe but fascinating passage from the book of Baruch (an ancient text not included in most Bibles) that says God will send the giants again in the last days as part of His judgment. We don't hang doctrine on that—but it's worth noting. Whether literal giants walk the earth again or not, the giant spirits of rebellion, pride, and violence are unmistakably back on the scene.

The question is: Will we recognize it for what it is?

Or will we, like the people of Noah's day, go on eating and drinking, marrying and giving in marriage, while the floodwaters rise around us?

THE ALIEN DECEPTION—A MODERN FACE FOR ANCIENT LIES

Let's talk about something that's been creeping in around the edges for a while now—the alien deception.

For decades, people have reported UFO sightings, strange abductions, crop circles, and encounters with beings that claim to be from other worlds. Governments have quietly collected data, pilots have come forward, and in recent years, the veil has started to lift:

"Yes, UFOs are real. We don't know what they are. We're investigating."

But let's be honest—they know exactly what they are.

These so-called "aliens" aren't visitors from another galaxy. They're spiritual beings—fallen angels, demonic entities, the same spirits that rebelled against God in Genesis 6 and took human wives. They're back, wearing a new mask for a modern age. What was once called Nephilim is now rebranded as extraterrestrials—but the agenda hasn't changed.

Here's the likely setup:

- They'll tell us they seeded life on earth.
- They'll say they've been guiding human evolution.
- They'll claim we're on the brink of a global awakening, and they're here to help us transcend.

It's the same old lie from the garden of Eden: "You will not surely die... you will be like God."

2 Thessalonians 2:9–11 warns us of a coming deception so powerful it will involve lying signs and wonders—and the alien narrative fits that bill perfectly. The world is being primed for a false savior narrative:

"Look! The aliens have come to save us! They'll end war, cure disease, reverse climate change... maybe even solve the riddle of death itself."

And the tragic part? Many will believe it. Even some in the Church may be swept up in it, especially if these other-worldly beings claim to have advanced knowledge of Jesus, or even present themselves as "ascended masters" or "higher beings" connected to Him.

We have to understand: this isn't science fiction. It's spiritual delusion, dressed up in high-tech packaging. The remnant needs to be ready—not just for the deception itself, but for the fallout when it comes.

So when the day arrives that world leaders and scientists step up to a microphone and say, "We've made contact"—don't be surprised. Be discerning. Be rooted. Be unshaken.

The Return of the 'Gods'

The old gods never really left. They just went underground—waiting for a moment like this. When we think of ancient gods like Baal, Molech, Ishtar, we imagine ancient statues, forgotten rituals, and crumbling temples. But those weren't just myths or relics. They were the faces of ancient spiritual powers—principalities and demons that demanded human sacrifice, perverted sexuality, and enslaved entire cultures. And now? They're reemerging.

Jonathan Cahn calls this the *Return of the Gods*, and I think he's onto something. We see Baal's influence in the obsession with power, control, and rebellion. We see Molech's spirit in the blood sacrifice of abortion—millions of innocent lives offered up on the altar of convenience. We see Ishtar's fingerprints all over the sexual chaos of our culture: the blurring of gender, the worship of pleasure, the desecration of marriage.

And just like in the days of old, people are unwittingly bowing down—

> These aren't just cultural shifts. They're spiritual revivals of ancient powers.

through media, entertainment, politics, and even some churches that have compromised the truth for the sake of relevance.

Psalm 82 gives us a window into this spiritual reality:

> *"God has taken his place in the divine council; in the midst of the gods he holds judgment... I said, 'You are gods, sons of the Most High, all of you; nevertheless, like men you shall die, and fall like any prince.'"*

These rebellious spirits—these so-called "gods"—know their time is short. They're not just influencing nations; they're conditioning hearts, dulling consciences, and preparing the world for the final deception.

But the remnant? We are called to see through the smoke and mirrors. We're called to expose the darkness and stand in the gap—to be the ones who say, "No, not here. Not on our watch."

DEMONIC MANIFESTATIONS AND LAWLESSNESS

As the end approaches, the spiritual temperature is rising. The darkness isn't hiding anymore—it's coming out in the open. We are going to see more and more demonic manifestations in the days ahead.

People tormented by voices they can't explain.

Physical attacks and spiritual oppression.

Strange phenomena in the skies, in homes, even in churches.

Open displays of witchcraft, pagan rituals, and dark ceremonies—not hidden in back rooms, but on public stages and social media feeds.

This isn't sensationalism. It's a spiritual forecast based on Scripture. Revelation 12:12 says:

"Woe to the earth and the sea, because the devil has gone down to you in great fury, because he knows that his time is short."

The enemy is desperate, and his strategy is simple: divide and conquer.

Lawlessness will increase—violence in the streets, chaos in homes, and the erosion of basic decency.

Racial tensions will be inflamed—not just in the world, but in the church.

Political factions will grow more hostile—left vs. right, rich vs. poor, liberal vs. conservative, Marxist vs. Capitalist...the list could on.

Fear will spread like a virus, pushing people into isolation, panic, and hopelessness, and even violence. **2 Timothy 3:1–5 (ESV)** warned us:

> *"But understand this, that in the last days there will come times of difficulty. For people will be lovers of self, lovers of money, proud, arrogant... disobedient to their parents, ungrateful, unholy... not loving good, treacherous, reckless, swollen with conceit, lovers of pleasure rather than lovers of God, having the appearance of godliness, but denying its power."*

Sound familiar? But here's the thing: we can't get swept up in it. The remnant has to stay laser-focused. Don't let the enemy bait you into fleshly battles—arguments over politics, race, or culture wars that pull you off mission.

Our battle is not flesh and blood. It's not about winning debates or proving a point. It's about fighting for souls. It's about standing in the gap for the lost, the broken, and the deceived. We're not called to fix the world's systems. We're called to shine as lights in the darkness, to proclaim the gospel, and to stand firm in love—even as the world careens toward the inevitable.

How Do We Respond?

The darkness is rising, the deceipt is deepening, and the enemy's tactics are getting bolder. So how do we, as the remnant, live in this tension?
How do we stay awake without becoming anxious?
How do we prepare without becoming paralyzed?
How do we fight without losing our focus?
Here's what I've learned—and I'm preaching to myself just as much as to you:

- **Stay focused on the mission.**
  Don't get distracted by every headline, every theory, every cultural firestorm. Yes, be aware—but don't let awareness become obsession. Our mission hasn't changed: Preach the gospel. Make disciples. Love people fiercely. Be the hands and feet of Jesus.

- **Be aware, but not afraid.**
  The enemy wants us consumed with fear—fear of the giants, fear of the aliens, fear of the collapse, and fear of the future. But fear is not our fuel.
  Faith is.
  Wisdom is.
  Bold love is.

The Rising Tide of Deception

- **Anchor in the Word, not the news.**
  Headlines shift. Propaganda spins. But the Word of God is unshakable. Build your worldview, your discernment, and your peace on what God says, not what the world shouts.

- **Let the Spirit lead your preparations.**
  There's no cookie-cutter formula. For some, it might mean storing food. For others, it's getting out of debt, learning a trade, or investing in community. For some, it's focusing on spiritual gifts and prayer.
  Ask the Lord: *What do YOU want me to focus on?*
  And trust that He will guide you.

- **Stay connected.**
  This isn't a solo mission. Find your tribe. Build community. Pray together. Discern together. Encourage each other when the days get dark.

- **Keep your eyes on Jesus.**
  The deception is strong—but the Light is stronger.
  The darkness is rising—but so is the remnant.
  We aren't just surviving—we're advancing the Kingdom in enemy territory. So stay the course. Don't give up. Don't grow weary. And don't let the darkness dim your fire.

Final Thought:

The storm is coming. The lies will multiply.
But the remnant will stand—not because we're strong, but because we belong to the One who is.
Let's be the ones who rise, who watch, who warn, and who shine—even when the world is falling apart.

Closing Prayer

Lord, In these days of deception and darkness,
open our eyes to see clearly.
Give us discernment to recognize
the schemes of the enemy—whether they come
dressed as political saviors, spiritual leaders,
or false signs and wonders.

Help us not to fear, but to stand firm
in the truth of Your Word.
Teach us how to live wisely in this world—
to be in it, but not of it.
Show us how to prepare, how to love, how to serve,
and how to shine as lights in the darkness.

**Help us to stay on mission, to bring Your Kingdom
wherever we go, and to never lose sight
of the ultimate goal: to glorify You.**

Strengthen us, Lord.
Keep us from distraction.
Guard us from fear.
And may we be found faithful—
watching, waiting, and standing firm
until the day You return.
In Jesus' name, Amen.

8

When the Weight of the World is Too Heavy

We can see the storm clouds gathering. The deception is rising, the spiritual battle is intensifying, and the darkness feels overwhelming. It's easy to get lost in the headlines, to feel consumed by the sheer weight of it all.

But beyond the strategies of the enemy and the systems of control, there's a deeper ache that we carry—a heart cry that groans under the weight of a broken and darkening world.

And that's where we must pause, reflect, and ask the harder questions:
Where is God in this?
Why does He allow such horror?
And how do we, as His remnant, respond when the burden feels too heavy to bear?

God's Heart: Grieved Beyond Measure

Sometimes, the weight of the world feels unbearable. The blood of the innocent cries out. The screams of children echo in the darkness. The news is too much to watch. The pain is too much to process. And we wonder...

Where is God? Is He indifferent?
Why does He seem to stand by while humans suffer the unspeakable?
Why are some spared while others are crushed beneath the wheels of evil?

These are not just intellectual questions; they're the cry of a soul that loves what God loves and hates what God hates.

Scripture tells us that God is not willing that any should perish (2 Peter 3:9). He does not delight in the death of the wicked (Ezekiel 33:11). He loves little children and says that anyone who harms them would be better off with a millstone tied around their neck (Matthew 18:6). His heart is grieved over sin, and His patience is not indifference—it's mercy, longing to save even the worst of sinners.

But the cup of iniquity is filling. And one day soon, it will overflow. Justice will come like a flood.

The Whisper of the Fallen

We are in the middle of a cosmic war. There is more happening than we can possibly see. Ephesians 6:12 tells us that we do not wrestle against flesh and blood, but against principalities, powers, and rulers of the darkness of this age.

The fallen realm whispers lies to the world's elite:

"You can be like gods."
"Depopulate the earth for the greater good."
"Destroy carbon, merge with AI, build a utopia without God."

But it is deception. They are pawns—"useful idiots" in the hands of the enemy, fueling a fire that will consume them. And like Haman in the book of Esther, they are building the very gallows on which they themselves will hang. They believe the lie, but they will be betrayed. What they construct in arrogance will become the instruments of their own undoing.

Why Some Live and Others Die

This is the hardest question of all. Some are miraculously spared—like Shadrach, Meshach, and Abednego in the fire. Others are martyred—like Stephen, stoned while heaven opened before him.

Why does God save some and not others?

The truth is, *God doesn't value survival above all else. He values faithfulness, testimony, and eternal impact.* Sometimes He allows His people to die as a witness to the world—and to the unseen realm. Sometimes He rescues for a future mission.

It's a mystery we won't fully understand this side of eternity, but we know this:

"Shall not the Judge of all the earth do right?" (Genesis 18:25)
"For now we see through a glass, darkly; but then face to face..." (1 Corinthians 13:12)

Why Does God Let the Wicked Continue?

This is Psalm 73's lament: *"Why do the wicked prosper?"* And yet, the psalmist concludes: *"Then I understood their end." (Psalm 73:17)*

God is longsuffering, but judgment is coming. The blood of the innocent cries out from the ground (Genesis 4:10). And one day, the Lamb will return as the Lion, and justice will be swift and sure.

FINAL COMFORT: THE LAMB WILL HAVE THE FINAL WORD

Revelation shows us the martyrs crying out: *"How long, O Lord?"* (Revelation 6:10). And God replies, *"Wait a little longer"* (Revelation 6:11). But then… the day comes. The Lamb returns. Evil is crushed. The righteous are vindicated. The war ends. The King reigns. And the little ones who suffered are safe forever in His arms. **The Lamb will have the final word.**

DEVOTIONAL REFLECTION:
WHEN THE WEIGHT OF THE WORLD IS TOO HEAVY

For now, we are the ones who feel the weight. We weep. We grieve. We carry the pain to the throne of grace, knowing that every tear is precious to Him.

We trust this:

> *"For the Lord is near to the brokenhearted and saves the crushed in spirit."*
> *(Psalm 34:18)*

> *You keep track of all my sorrows. You have collected all my tears in your bottle. You have recorded each one in your book.*
> *Psalm 56:8 (NLT)*

The cross was the ultimate injustice—and yet it was also the place where justice and mercy kissed. So we cling to the cross, even when we don't understand. We grieve—but we grieve with hope. We fight—but we fight with love. We wait—but we wait with faith.

Psalm of Lament: A Cry for the Innocent

Oh Lord, how long will You wait?
How long will the blood of the innocent stain the earth?
The cries of the little ones echo in the darkness,
and my soul cannot bear it.
Their tiny hands, torn and broken.
Their lives, stolen and crushed.

You are the God who sees—But why do You not
strike down the wicked in their tracks?
Why do You let the traffickers prosper,
the abusers flourish,
the murderers breathe another day?

Lord, my heart is raw with grief.
I cannot comprehend Your ways.
I trust You, but I am crushed
under the weight of this pain.
How long, O Lord? How long?

Yet I will remember:
You are not slow to act, as some count slowness.
You are not willing that any should perish,
but that all should come to repentance.

But woe to those who harden their hearts.
Woe to those who shed innocent blood.
For the day of the Lord will come like a thief,
and none will escape Your justice.

Until that day, strengthen me, Lord.
Help me stand in the gap for the vulnerable.
Help me weep with those who weep,
pray for those who suffer,
and speak truth in the darkness.

Give me faith to trust that
You will wipe away every tear—
and that the little ones You have gathered
into Your arms are safe forever in Your kingdom.
In Jesus' name, Amen.

In the Ages to Come

There is more happening than we can possibly see. More than the wars, the elections, the crises, or the tears we shed today.

God's plan of redemption—the plan that sent Jesus to earth, the plan that took Him to the cross, the plan that raised Him from the dead—isn't just about our lives here and now.

It is a story that will echo through the ages to come.

Ephesians 2:7 says that God's purpose is to demonstrate the immeasurable riches of His grace in the coming ages.

This means that the salvation of a single soul, the faithfulness of a single saint, the suffering of a single martyr, the worship of a single child—all of it ripples across eternity.

The victory of the cross is not a footnote in history. It is the centerpiece of the ages, the cosmic reversal of sin's curse, the triumphant declaration that Jesus is Lord—not just of earth, but of the unseen realms.

When we choose obedience in the small things…

When we hold fast to Jesus in the hard things…

When we shine light in the darkness…

we are part of a story that will echo into eternity.

> *The cross was the ultimate injustice—yet it was the place where justice and mercy kissed.*

9

THE SCRIPTED DECEPTION: WHEN HEROES WEAR COSTUMES

THE DISORIENTING REALIZATION

Shakespeare once wrote, "All the world's a stage, and all the men and women merely players."

Elvis echoed the sentiment in his ballad "Are You Lonesome Tonight," describing life as a script we each perform.

But what if the 'world stage' isn't just poetic metaphor? What if it's a reality—carefully cast, choreographed, and controlled?

What if some of the most charismatic leaders—those who rally the crowds and make freedom-loving people cheer—are actually part of the plan? What if their role is not to save us but to soften us? Not to resist the system, but to deliver the remnant into it?

These aren't easy questions to ask. But if we're going to walk in discernment, we can't afford to be dazzled by optics. We need to ask hard questions, even about those we admire. *Especially* about those we admire.

Because sometimes, the hero is wearing a costume.

I've wrestled with this idea privately for a while now. Something about the direction of current events just doesn't add up. On the surface, it looks like things

> *If Satan can masquerade as an angel of light, why would we think his agents couldn't wear red, white, and blue?*

are being corrected—corrupt agencies being exposed, illegal operations being dismantled, borders being enforced. Conservative Americans and Christians are breathing a cautious sigh of relief.

But what if it's **bait**?

What if this is part of a larger deception so deep, so sophisticated, that even the elect would be deceived if it were possible (see Matthew 24:24)?

The World as a Stage—Even Now?

It's hard to admit we might be watching a script. But we need to.

We're living in a time where image outweighs integrity, optics override truth, and perception management is a science. The news isn't just reporting what happens. It's crafting a narrative. And in that narrative, characters are carefully cast, and the mockingbird media repeats the same lines.

2 Corinthians 11:13–14 reminds us:

> *"For such men are false apostles, deceitful workmen, disguising themselves as apostles of Christ. And no wonder, for even Satan disguises himself as an angel of light."*

False Hope as a Trap

Here's the uncomfortable truth: The only way to get the freedom-loving, truth-seeking remnant to go along with The Great Reset is to present a hero who appears to oppose it.

That's the Hegelian Dialectic in action:

Problem: Chaos, corruption, lawlessness.

Reaction: "We must have someone strong to restore order!"

Solution: A pre-selected leader with a pre-approved agenda, dressed up as the answer to the problem.

It feels like deliverance. It sounds like freedom. But it leads to deeper control.

The Scripted Deception: When Heroes Wear Costumes

Predictive Programming and Political Redesign

When I heard the idea floating around of making Canada the 51st state or adding Greenland as U.S. territory, my antenna went up.

On the surface, it sounded bold and patriotic. But dig deeper and find that it aligns with longstanding globalist goals: the North American Union, and ultimately, the division of the world into ten regional kingdoms like those prophesied in Daniel 7 and Revelation 17.

This is how predictive programming works:

- Float the idea.
- Wrap it in humor or patriotism.
- Normalize it through repetition.
- By the time it becomes reality, resistance is gone.

It's not about national strength. It's about global control.

Controlled Opposition: When Your Champion Is the Setup

One administration allows migrants to pour across the border unchecked. The next administration begins rounding up illegal aliens and shipping them to offshore detention centers. The public cheers: "Finally! Someone is taking action!" It appears as if the two administrations are in stark opposition—but the contrast was scripted from the beginning.

But what if that's only Phase One?

First: remove the obvious lawbreakers.

Next: redefine who is dangerous.

Finally: target anyone who opposes the narrative.

And by then? The system is built. The infrastructure is in place. And the public already applauded it.

This is how liberty is lost: not by a sudden takeover, but by strategic deception that feels like deliverance.

Unmasking the Show

In the world of professional wrestling, there's a term called kayfabe. It refers to the scripted illusion that the wrestlers are bitter enemies fighting for honor, revenge, or championship gold. In reality, many of them are friends behind the scenes—rehearsing their moves, planning dramatic betrayals, and even traveling together after the show.

But to preserve the manufactured reality, they keep up the act even off camera. Because if fans saw the two "enemies" laughing in a limo after a brutal grudge match, they'd feel betrayed. They paid to believe the storyline. And the wrestlers know: if the illusion breaks, the control breaks.

It's not unlike watching a movie like *Superman*. We all know it's fiction. We know Clark Kent didn't really fly to Earth from Krypton. But for two hours, we suspend our disbelief. We sit in a dark theater and let ourselves be transported. The music swells, the dialogue moves us, and for a while—it feels real.

> *It's not about fooling the mind. It's about captivating the heart just long enough to keep the illusion alive.*

Movie studios spend hundreds of millions to make sure nothing looks cheesy or fake. They want us emotionally invested. They want us to believe, even though we know it's fiction.

That's the power of kayfabe:
It's not about fooling the mind.
It's about captivating the heart just long enough to keep the illusion alive.

Now take that same principle... and apply it to the world stage.

What if much of modern politics operates on the same script?

What if the left and the right are characters, not combatants—rivals on screen, allies behind the curtain?

We've seen it play out:

- One administration mandates injections and pushes a global health pass. The next promises freedom—but never dismantles the emergency powers or the surveillance infrastructure left behind. The appearance of change keeps the public pacified while the system quietly strengthens.

This is national-level kayfabe.

A scripted illusion designed not to inform you—but to shape your loyalties, stir your emotions, and keep you distracted while the true agenda marches on.

> *The enemy doesn't need you to believe a lie.*
> *He just needs you emotionally invested in the script*
> *long enough to stop asking questions.*

The Scripted Deception: When Heroes Wear Costumes

The remnant must step outside the theater. Outside the ring. Outside the carefully controlled opposition. And ask:
Who's writing the script—and why do they want me to play along?
What do they want to distract my attention from?
What scandal or inconvenient truth disappeared the moment this new crisis took center stage?

Prophets, Puppets, and Political Theater

It's painful to say, but it must be said: Some of the spiritual voices we've trusted may have been co-opted. Others may have been planted from the start.

If the enemy masquerades as an angel of light, his servants will too.

The Book of Revelation warns us of a beast with two horns like a lamb, but who speaks like a dragon (Revelation 13:11). In other words, it appears Christlike... but its message betrays its true nature.

Some public figures name-drop Jesus, quote Scripture, and even pray on stage. But their fruit reveals their allegiance. Therefore, **we can no longer afford to be naive. This is the age of infiltration.**

Prepping for Betrayal: How Do We Stand?

The betrayal of trust is one of the hardest trials to endure. It shakes your foundation. It tempts you to despair. But God hasn't left us unprepared. Scripture is filled with warnings—not so we'll live in fear, but so we'll walk in truth.

Therefore, what do we do?

- **Stay spiritually alert.** Test everything. Compare every message to Scripture. Be slow to cheer for any political savior.
- **Anchor yourself in God's Word.** Not in headlines. Not in headlines disguised as prophecy. In the living, breathing Word of God.
- **Train your discernment.** Help others see through the fog. Speak the truth in love. Let your life be an example of steadfastness in an age of instability.
- **Prepare your heart.** We will be betrayed by people we trusted. Some may fall away. Some may turn. But the Lord is faithful, and He will never leave us.
- **Remember the real battle.** It's not Left vs. Right. It's not conservative vs. progressive. *It's truth vs. deception. Light vs. darkness.*

Don't just prepare for hard times. Prepare for hard truths.

Prayer for Discernment

Lord, open our eyes to see clearly
in this age of illusion.
Give us discernment to recognize deception,
even when it wears the face of a hero.

Help us discern not just deception
in the world—but deception in ourselves.
Help us walk in truth and anchor
our hope in You alone.

Strengthen us to endure betrayal
without bitterness and to stand firm
when others fall away.

Keep us faithful, awake, and
aligned with Your will—no matter
whatthe world applauds.
In Jesus' name, Amen.

10

WHOSE KINGDOM ARE YOU WATCHING FOR?

The world is moving fast—shifting, shaking, changing.
Nations are aligning.
Economies are trembling.
Technology is accelerating at a dizzying pace.
And in the midst of it all, many believers are asking:
"Where is all of this heading?"
We see corrupt leaders overriding the will of the people.
We watch societies hurtling toward tyranny at breakneck speed.
And sometimes, it feels like there's nothing we can do to stop it.
But here's the truth the remnant must remember:
The kingdoms of this world are temporary.
The Kingdom of Christ is eternal.
It's tempting to get caught up in political battles, to fixate on global leaders, or to anxiously watch the news cycles for signs of collapse. But the real question for the remnant is this:

Whose Kingdom are you watching for?

Because no matter how chaotic the kingdoms of men become, there is another Kingdom—a higher Kingdom—that will not be shaken.

Yes, the powers of darkness are scheming. Yes, they will have their brief moment of dominance. Scripture tells us plainly that a false messiah will arise, deceive the nations, and lead many astray.

But the Bible also tells us what happens next:

Jesus returns.

Not as the suffering servant—but as the conquering King.

When He comes, He will establish a true and righteous order:

No more injustice.

No more oppression.

No more tears, sickness, or death.

No more thrones built on lies and blood.

> *"The kingdom of the world has become the kingdom of our Lord and of His Christ; and He will reign forever and ever."*
> *— Revelation 11:15*

That is the *real* "New World Order." The one our hearts long for. The one we are citizens of even now.

A Tale of Two Kingdoms

Throughout Scripture, two kingdoms are always in conflict: the kingdom of God and the kingdoms of this world.

Pharaoh vs. Moses.

Nebuchadnezzar vs. Daniel.

Herod vs. Jesus.

The Beast vs. the Lamb.

The conflict is cosmic.

The stakes are eternal.

And the battle lines are drawn not just in governments or nations—but in the hearts of individuals.

The remnant must constantly choose:

Will we anchor our hope in temporary systems, or in the everlasting King?

The Perils of Unpreparedness

History offers a sobering reminder of what happens when God's people are taught to expect ease instead of endurance.

In the mid-20th century, the Chinese Church was thriving. Many believers were taught a comforting eschatology — that Jesus would rapture them away before any major suffering occurred. Hopeful and trusting, they believed they would be spared from the brutal realities of tribulation.

But then came the Communist Revolution. Bibles were confiscated. Churches were burned. Pastors were imprisoned or killed. Christians faced horrific persecution — and the promised escape never came.

The betrayal they felt wasn't just at the hands of the Communist regime. It was the crushing disillusionment of realizing that their faith had been built, at least partially, on an expectation of escape, rather than an assurance of endurance.

We must learn from their pain.

Today in the Western Church, many still cling to a singular view of end-time events — particularly the pre-tribulation rapture — with little room for alternative perspectives. But what if persecution arises before that day comes? What if hardship touches us, as it already has so many of our brothers and sisters around the world? Would our faith crumble under unmet expectations? Or would we be anchored — come what may — in the unshakable reality of Christ?

This historical event in China underscores the peril of holding rigidly to a single end-times viewpoint. Being overly dogmatic can leave believers unprepared for suffering, leading to crises of faith when trials arise.

Corrie ten Boom,
a Holocaust survivor and faithful witness, recounted:

In China, the Christians were told, "Don't worry, before the tribulation comes you will be translated—raptured." Then came a terrible persecution. Millions of Christians were tortured to death. Later I heard a Bishop from China say, sadly, "We have failed. *We should have made the people strong for persecution*, rather than telling them Jesus would come first."

STANDING READY—NO MATTER THE SEQUENCE

Whether Jesus calls us home before tribulation, during it, or after it, the commission remains the same:

- To endure in faith.
- To overcome by the blood of the Lamb and the word of our testimony.
- To be faithful witnesses — even in the face of fire.

> *Better to be surprised by the rapture than by the Tribulation. Build your faith for either—anchored in Christ alone.*

Jesus Himself warned, *"Here on earth you will have many trials and sorrows. But take heart, because I have overcome the world"* — *John 16:33 (NLT).*

The remnant must prepare not merely for escape — but for endurance. We are not guaranteed exemption from suffering. But we are guaranteed His presence through it. And that—*that*—is the anchor that will hold when the storm breaks and the whirlwind howls.

EYES FIXED ON THE TRUE KINGDOM

As believers, we are called to be awake, alert, and aware of the times.
But awareness is different from obsession.
Awareness points us to preparedness.
Obsession pulls us into panic or passivity.
We are not watching simply for the Antichrist.
We are watching for the return of the King.
We are not living in fear of the beast system.
We are living in anticipation of the Lion of Judah.

The remnant must keep eyes and hearts trained upward—so that no matter how thick the darkness becomes, we are drawn ever toward the coming dawn.

Paul admonished us: *"Focus your minds on the things above, not on things here on earth."* — *Colossians 3:2 (CJB)*

It doesn't mean we ignore what's happening on Earth; it means we view everything through a higher lens. We live awake, but not afraid. Alert, but anchored. Grieved by evil, but glowing with hope. Because no matter what the news says, no matter how dark the headlines grow: **Jesus wins.**

Closing Charge: Commissioned to Watch

Stay awake. Stay anchored. Stay ablaze.
Watch not just the signs of the times, but the Author of them.
His Kingdom is coming. His Kingdom cannot fail.
And you, dear remnant, were born for such a time as this.

Prayer for the Watchful Remnant

*Lord Jesus,
In a world obsessed with power and panic,
Fix my eyes on Your Kingdom.
Let me not be drawn into the chaos of the day,
But anchored in the certainty of Your return.*

*Help me to live awake, alert, and faithful—
Not just watching for signs,
But waiting for You.
Establish Your Kingdom in my heart,
And let my life reflect
the One who is coming.*
Amen.

Remnant Rising

11

COME OUT OF HER MY PEOPLE

"Then I heard another voice out of heaven say: "My people, come out of her!
so that you will not share in her sins, so that you will not be infected by her plagues"
— Revelation 18:4 (CJB)

"Therefore, come out from their midst and be separate, says the Lord.
And do not touch what is unclean; and I will welcome you and I will be a father to you,
and you shall be sons and daughters to Me," says the Lord Almighty.
— 2 Corinthians 6:17–18

This is not the hour to blend in. This is not the time to salvage Babylon. Her systems are crumbling by design. Her glittering promises are poison. Her towers of progress are built on blood and deception. The remnant isn't called to patch her walls with optimism or whitewash her corruption with nationalism, religion, or reform.

Babylon represents a spiritual system that has existed since the Tower of Babel: rebellion wrapped in advancement. It's a counterfeit kingdom, a seductive network of politics, wealth, commerce, entertainment, and even compromised religion. She enslaves minds, whispers lies, and lures hearts into apathy. Babylon has many faces, but one agenda: to draw humanity away from allegiance to the true King.

The remnant is awakening. The call to "Come out of her" is more than a poetic cry—it is a divine summons to separate, to sanctify, and to live as those who belong to a different kingdom entirely.

What Does It Mean to "Come Out" of Babylon?

To come out of her doesn't mean you leave society and live in a bunker (unless God tells you to!). It means:

- ❖ **Refusing to participate** in her moral decay and ideological delusion.
- ❖ **Choosing holiness** when compromise is trendy.
- ❖ **Rejecting allegiance** to the beast systems that elevate man above God.
- ❖ **Detaching your identity** from career, politics, wealth, or even Christian celebrity culture.
- ❖ **Standing as a witness** against her practices, even when it costs you friends, comfort, or platforms.

Coming out is not isolation—it's consecration. It's saying, "I belong to another Kingdom."

Babylon Is Falling

Revelation doesn't say Babylon *might* fall. It says she *will*.

"Fallen, fallen is Babylon the Great!" — *Revelation 18:2*

Every deceptive structure—from corrupt media and compromised institutions to occult-influenced entertainment and globalist agendas—will fall. The only question is whether God's people will be rescued from her or entangled with her when the collapse comes. **This is a mercy call. A trumpet blast. Not a warning of fear, but a summons to freedom.**

> *We are not here to save Babylon. We are here to call people out of her.*

What the Remnant Must Do

1. **Discern the times.** Don't sleep through the shaking. Ask the Holy Spirit to expose Babylon's fingerprints in your life.
2. **Live visibly different.** Be a contrast. Your lifestyle should preach louder than your Instagram.
3. **Speak with clarity.** Not with rage or self-righteousness, but with bold, Spirit-led urgency.
4. **Rescue others.** You are not just leaving Babylon—you are helping others escape too.
5. **Anchor yourself in the Kingdom.** Now is the time to worship, pray, and root yourself in eternal truth.

The remnant doesn't whisper in Babylon's halls.
They cry out from the wilderness,
"Make straight the way of the Lord."

The remnant doesn't just cry out, "Make straight the way of the Lord"—they live in such a way that clears the path. In ancient times, when a king prepared to travel, servants would go ahead to clear the road—removing debris, smoothing rough places, and making the path ready. That's what it meant to "make straight the way of the Lord." It wasn't metaphorical. It was prophetic preparation.

In similar fashion, we are called to do the same today—not with shovels, not with shofars, but with obedience. One of the most overlooked ways we prepare the road is by aligning our lives with His calendar. God's appointed times are not empty rituals—they're markers on a map. Mileposts of meaning. And just as John the Baptist heralded the first coming of the King, the remnant today is being awakened to the *moedim* of His return: His appointed feasts.

Moedim: God's Appointed Times

The Hebrew word "moedim" (מוֹעֲדִים) means appointed times.' These are not just Jewish holidays, they are divine appointments set by God Himself to reveal His redemptive plan. Each feast points to a major event in the story of salvation:

Passover (Pesach) – The Lamb is slain (Jesus' crucifixion)
Unleavened Bread – The sinless body in the tomb
Firstfruits – The resurrection
Pentecost (Shavuot) – The outpouring of the Spirit
Trumpets (Yom Teruah) – The return of the King
Day of Atonement (Yom Kippur) – Final judgment and mercy
Tabernacles (Sukkot) – God dwelling with us

These are not burdens, they're blessings. Reminders. Rehearsals. Prophetic previews of what was, what is, and what is still to come.

*The feasts aren't rituals—
they're rehearsals of redemption.*

Obedience in an Age of Deception: Rediscovering Covenant Faithfulness

Coming out of Babylon isn't just about exiting a corrupt system—it's about entering into covenant with the King. It's not enough to say, "I reject the world," if we're still living like it.

Babylon may have fallen, but she's still persuasive. She still whispers compromise in the ears of those who call themselves God's people. If we want to stand distinct in the final hour, we must return to the simplicity of loving God His way.

1. Grace Isn't New—It's Eternal

Some have wrongly divided Scripture as if the "Old Testament" was all law and judgment, and the "New Testament" suddenly introduced grace. But God's grace didn't begin with Jesus—it's been there from Eden. The Hebrew word *chesed* (חֶסֶד) describes His lovingkindness and mercy throughout the Psalms, the prophets, and even the wilderness journey.

The cross didn't change God's character. It revealed it. Jesus didn't come to abolish the Torah—He came to fulfill it (Matthew 5:17). That means He brought it to its full meaning, not to erase it. The grace that saves us is the same grace that empowers us to walk in obedience.

2. Obedience Isn't Legalism—It's Love

Keeping God's commandments isn't about working our way to heaven. It's about living in alignment with the One we love. Think of a couple in love. When you're dating, you put your best foot forward. You learn what brings the other joy. You listen, you honor, you adjust. Then comes marriage—not the end of pursuit, but the deepening of it. Love doesn't stop at "I do." It shows up in the daily choosing.

Jesus said plainly: *"If you love Me, keep My commandments."* —John 14:15

And again: *"Whoever keeps and teaches them shall be called great in the kingdom of heaven."* —Matthew 5:19

He wasn't issuing burdens. He was describing covenant loyalty.

3. Sabbath Still Matters

God set apart the seventh day from the very beginning as a pattern to emulate —not as a burden, but as a blessing and a sign.

> *"...this is a sign between me and you through all your generations; so that you will know that I am Adonai, who sets you apart for me." —Exodus 31:13 (CJB)*

The Sabbath—from Friday sundown to Saturday sundown—was never changed by God. Its purpose wasn't erased by the resurrection. Honoring the rhythm of God's creation becomes even more vital as the world accelerates into chaos.

This isn't about legalism. It's about distinction. The Holy Spirit may lead each believer differently, but the remnant must be willing to ask: "Lord, is there something You're asking me to realign?"

4. Traditions or Truth?

This one might sting. But love must be willing to ask uncomfortable questions.

Jesus was crucified during Passover, buried during Unleavened Bread, and rose on Firstfruits—God's appointed feasts, not man-made holidays. So why do we continue to tether ourselves to Babylonian-rooted traditions like Easter and Christmas, along with colored eggs and flying reindeer?

This isn't about condemning celebration. It's about asking the Holy Spirit, *"Am I participating in something that grieves Your heart?"* Some may continue in these traditions with clear conscience. Others may feel called to separate entirely. *There is no judgment here*—only an invitation to seek the Lord sincerely.

5. The Wise Virgins Had Oil

Jesus told a sobering parable: ten virgins awaited the Bridegroom. All were invited. All had lamps. But only five had oil when He arrived.

Oil speaks of intimacy, preparation, and covenant.

The wise ones didn't just say yes to the invitation—they prepared to meet Him. In Hebrew wedding custom, a Ketubah (marriage covenant) was signed between bride and groom. It was more than emotion—it was commitment. It was "I am Yours—and I will be ready when You come."

Let the remnant say the same.

FINAL WORDS: OBEY BECAUSE YOU ARE LOVED

Salvation is a gift—we don't earn it by commandment-keeping. But the one who loves will desire to obey. James reminds us that faith without works is *dead* faith, not *living* faith. And 1 John says that God's commands are not burdensome. The remnant cannot afford a lazy, casual faith that waves a banner of grace while trampling on covenant.

I say this not to condemn, but to call. As one who will be held accountable for what I teach, I would rather err on the side of wholehearted obedience than diluted compromise. Not to impress God—but to reflect that I am His.

Hope for the Called-Out Ones

You may feel alone. Exiled. Mocked. But the same voice that calls you out also calls you His own. He is gathering a bride who has made herself ready. Not stained by Babylon's excess. Not drunk on her delusion. Not lulled to sleep by her entertainment and distractions.

You were born for this.

You are not a reformer of Babylon. You are an ambassador of a coming Kingdom—a watchment, a warrior.

And your cry matters.

> *Come out of her, My people. Be marked by My Name.*
> *And shine like stars in the darkness. For the hour is late,*
> *but the light in you is Mine.*

Remnant Rising

12

Walking in Kingdom Power in Dark Times

We were never called to survive the darkness. We were called to push it back. When Jesus said, "You are the light of the world," He wasn't offering a compliment—He was issuing a commission. And light doesn't hide. It shines, even when the night grows thick. In fact, that's when it shines best.

Kingdom Power Was Never Optional

The early Church wasn't built on clever sermons or flashy programs. It wasn't built on comfort or convenience or cultural approval.
It was built on power.
Power that healed the sick.
Power that cast out demons.
Power that raised the dead.
Power that emboldened fearful men to preach without apology—even under threat of death.

"For the kingdom of God is not a matter of talk, but of power."
—*1 Corinthians 4:20*

In other words, we weren't saved to sit quietly. We were filled to function supernaturally as citizens of a Kingdom that overrides the systems of this world.

That Same Power Lives in You

The same Spirit that hovered over the waters at creation…
The same Spirit that descended on Jesus like a dove…
The same Spirit that raised Christ from the grave…
Now lives in you.

> *"You will receive power when the Holy Spirit has come upon you; and you shall be My witnesses…"* —Acts 1:8

This is not poetic language. It's not reserved for "special" Christians.

WHY DO SO MANY BELIEVERS FEEL POWERLESS?

We quote the verses.
We sing the songs.
We read about miracles and courage and unshakable faith…
But many believers—if they're being honest—feel disconnected from Kingdom power. Not just occasionally. Consistently.
It's like having a well with no bucket.
A lamp with no oil.
A weapon with no will to wield it.
And the reasons? They vary, but here are a few that show up time and again:

1. **We've Settled for Head Knowledge Without Heart Fire**

    It's possible to believe all the right things about God and yet live without vital connection to Him.
    We've been taught to study, but not always to surrender.
    We've been trained to analyze, but not always to abide.
    We know the Word; but do we know the Voice?
    Power doesn't come from knowledge alone. It comes from communion. You can memorize every miracle in Scripture and still live a powerless life if your faith isn't activated by intimacy. This has been true since the earliest days of the Church:

    - **In John 6, Jesus** spoke hard truth, and many who had followed Him could no longer accept His words. *"This is a hard saying. Who can listen to it?" (v. 60)*. They had walked with the Truth Himself—and

- yet turned back. Their minds were intrigued, but their hearts were not surrendered.

- **Judas** followed Jesus for three years. He heard every parable, saw every miracle, broke bread with the Bread of Life—and still betrayed Him with a kiss.

- **Alexander the coppersmith**, once a professing believer, later opposed Paul and the gospel. Head knowledge didn't hold him when pressure mounted.

- **Ananias and Sapphira** were part of the early church movement, but they cared more about appearing generous than about being honest. They believed in the power, but weren't transformed by the Presence.

- **In 1 John 2:19**, we see a pattern that still repeats today: *"They went out from us, but they were not really of us…"* They had the appearance of belonging, but lacked the internal fire that lasts when storms come.

So many start well. But it's the heart that keeps burning. Head knowledge may get you into the crowd, but only heart fire will keep you faithful in the chaos.

2. We're Afraid of What the Power Might Cost Us

Let's be honest: Kingdom power is disruptive. It's glorious, yes. But it's also dangerous. It exposes things. It challenges comfort. It costs something. Jesus didn't sugarcoat the price.

> *"For which one of you, when he wants to build a tower, does not first sit down and calculate the cost…?"* —Luke 14:28

To follow Jesus—to truly walk in His power—means dying to self, laying down reputation, and living with holy reverence. The early Church knew this all too well. After Ananias and Sapphira were struck dead for lying to the Holy Spirit:

> *"Great fear came over the whole church, and over all who heard of these things… but none of the rest dared to associate with them, however, the people held them in high esteem."* —Acts 5:11–13

In other words, the miracles didn't stop; but the casual observers did. People respected the power; but they also feared what it might require of them.

That same tension still exists today. We want the miracles, but are we willing to walk in the kind of holiness that sustains them? We want the anointing, but are we willing to surrender the parts of ourselves that would defile it? Sometimes the reason we don't walk in power is because we're more committed to comfort than we are to calling.

3. **We've Been Unplugged by Distraction, Disappointment, or Doubt**

The enemy doesn't always need to destroy your faith—he just needs to distract you from feeding it. Jesus told a parable of four types of soil. The seed—the Word of God—fell among thorns in one of them:

> *"And the worry of the world and the deceitfulness of wealth choke the word, and it becomes unfruitful." —Matthew 13:22*

That's the modern condition for many believers.
Not hostile to God.
Not rejecting truth.
Just choked. Overwhelmed. Numbed. Distracted.
Then there's doubt. Thomas walked with Jesus, yet questioned the resurrection until he saw proof. Many today live with paralyzed faith, waiting for a sign before they'll move forward in obedience.
And don't forget disappointment. Martha was busy serving, burdened by the pressures around her. Jesus looked at her and said:

> *"Martha, Martha, you are worried and bothered about so many things…"—Luke 10:41*

It wasn't sin that kept Martha from intimacy—it was stress. That same stress clogs the spiritual arteries of believers every day. In Revelation 2, Jesus praised the church at Ephesus for their endurance, their sound doctrine, their refusal to tolerate evil;

> *"But I have this against you, that you have left your first love."*

They were doing everything right, but something was still missing. The passion. The hunger. The fire.

Distraction. Doubt. Disappointment.
These are the silent saboteurs of Kingdom power. But they don't have to win. Sometimes all it takes is one moment of surrender, one cry of "Lord, rekindle the fire in me," and the plug is reconnected, the oil is replenished, and the flame begins to burn again.

WHAT KINGDOM POWER LOOKS LIKE WHEN IT'S PRESENT

When Kingdom power is alive in a believer, it's not just a feeling. It's not hype. It's not showmanship. It's evidence. It's heaven touching earth through surrendered vessels—not for personal glory, but for God's purposes. So what does that look like?

HOW KINGDOM POWER MANIFESTS IN THE SPIRIT-FILLED LIFE

When we stay connected to the True Vine, Kingdom power flows, and it looks like:

- **Boldness to Speak Truth:** Like Peter at Pentecost (Acts 2).
- **Discernment in Deception:** Like Paul confronting false apostles (2 Corinthians 11).
- **Miraculous Intervention:** Like the healings and signs in the early Church (Acts 5:12-16).
- **Supernatural Endurance:** Like Stephen while being stoned to death forgiving his executioners (Acts 7).
- **Joy in Suffering:** Like Paul and Silas singing hymns in prison (Acts 16).

This power isn't man-made hype; it's Spirit-breathed reality.

BIBLICAL AND MODERN EXAMPLES OF THE SPIRIT-FILLED LIFE

Boldness: William Wilberforce, fueled by the Spirit, campaigned for decades to abolish the slave trade—despite immense opposition.

Discernment: Corrie Ten Boom and her family hid Jews during WWII because they discerned the times—and their responsibility.

Miraculous Provision: Missionaries like George Müller ran orphanages purely by prayer and saw supernatural provision daily.

Unyielding Joy: Richard Wurmbrand, imprisoned and tortured for his faith, still rejoiced in Christ underground.

A Personal Story: When I Ignored the Spirit's Warning

When we sold our house in obedience to God's call to move, we made a good profit—and wanted to steward it wisely. My husband was following a well-known financial expert online and left a comment under one of his videos. Someone claiming to be that expert reached out. He sounded convincing. He offered a "high-yield investment opportunity."

From the start, I felt uneasy. Red flags popped up everywhere. My spirit twisted in discomfort. I knew something wasn't right. I told my husband I wasn't at peace about it; but he wanted so much to make our financial situation secure. Wanting to honor my husband's excitement, I silenced that inner alarm, reasoning that it was my natural skepticism rather than the Spirit's warning.

We wired the money. It was a scam. We lost nearly everything we had gained from the sale, and are still suffering the consequences financially. I should have trusted the Holy Spirit's prompting and my own gut-feeling. I learned the hard way that discernment ignored is discernment lost. Now, I listen. Now, I obey—even when it's uncomfortable.

Final Charge: Fan Into Flame the Gift of God

Paul wrote to Timothy:

> *"For this reason I remind you to fan into flame the gift of God, which is in you through the laying on of my hands."* (2 Timothy 1:6)

You were not saved to sit safely. You were saved to walk in Kingdom power. Fan the flame. Stoke the embers. Refuse to settle for a powerless life. The same Spirit that raised Christ from the dead lives in you.
Live like it.

13

Fit for the Fight

The remnant cannot afford to be spiritually sluggish.

We live in a time when evil is accelerating, deception is multiplying, and resistance to the truth is growing more intense by the day. Yet so many believers are caught off guard—scrambling to pray only after the battle breaks out, seeking Scripture only when a crisis erupts.

But warriors don't train in the middle of the war.

They prepare in advance.

Jesus modeled this. He often withdrew to solitary places to pray. He fasted for forty days before launching His public ministry. He stayed in constant communion with the Father so that when crowds pressed in, accusations rose up, or demons confronted Him, He was already fortified in Spirit.

He didn't wait until the storm hit.

He was ready when it came.

This kind of spiritual readiness is possible—but it's not accidental.

This Kind Comes Out Only by Prayer and Fasting

In Matthew 17, Jesus comes down from the mountain of transfiguration and finds His disciples unable to cast out a demon from a tormented boy.

They had authority—but not the readiness.

When they asked why they had failed, Jesus replied, *"This kind does not go out except by prayer and fasting." (Matthew 17:21, NKJV)*

The implication? Some breakthroughs require prior preparation.

You can't microwave your faith in a moment of emergency.

You must cultivate it consistently—before the need arises.

Everyday Analogies of Readiness

We see this principle all around us.

A farmer doesn't wait until the harvest season to start preparing. Long before any seed is planted, he tills the ground, removes rocks, pulls weeds, and enriches the soil. And after planting, he doesn't sit back passively. He waters, watches, protects, prunes.

Fruitfulness is work.

Readiness is cultivated.

A mother-to-be doesn't wait until contractions start to gather supplies. She eats well, gets rest, prepares the nursery, and readies her heart for the day of delivery. She's preparing now for what's coming later.

A firefighter doesn't wait for the blaze before learning how to handle a hose. He trains, drills, suits up, and stays ready—because when the call comes, there's no time to study.

The Minutemen of the American Revolutionary War were a select group of colonial militia trained to be ready at a minute's notice. They didn't wait until battle erupted to gather their weapons—they lived in a state of constant readiness. Their preparation, discipline, and swift response made a decisive impact during key moments of conflict.

Likewise, the remnant must prepare in advance.

Early Believers Who Escaped the Siege

In Luke 21:20–21, Jesus warned His followers: *"When you see Jerusalem surrounded by armies, then recognize that her desolation is near. Then those who are in Judea must flee to the mountains."*

Early church history suggests that many in the Messianic community remembered this prophecy. When they saw the Roman armies approaching in 66 A.D., they fled Jerusalem and relocated to a region called Pella, beyond the Jordan River. By heeding Jesus' words in advance, they escaped the horrific destruction that overtook the city in 70 A.D.

They didn't wait to obey.

They remembered—and responded.

A Culture of Complacency

The modern church often promotes comfort over conditioning. We've exchanged perseverance for positivity. We've replaced fasting with feasting. We've neglected spiritual disciplines until we desperately need them.

But the times demand more. We are not just called to be spiritually aware. We are called to be spiritually ready. Paul urged Timothy,

> *"Preach the word; be ready in season and out of season." (2 Timothy 4:2)*

> *If we want to love like God... Have patience like God... Be faithful and kind like God... Then we must be rooted in God.*

Peter wrote, *"Prepare your minds for action." (1 Peter 1:13)*

Preparation is not panic. It's wisdom. It's not fear-based—it's faith-fueled.

Practical Ways to Stay Spiritually Fit

- **Daily time in the Word** — Not just for information, but transformation.
- **Regular fasting** — Not as ritual, but to stay spiritually sharp.
- **Praying in the Spirit** — Building up your inner man (Jude 1:20).
- **Surrounding yourself with the prepared** — Iron sharpens iron.
- **Obedience in small things** — So you're ready for the big things.
- **Practicing rest** — Sabbath is preparation. Fatigue is vulnerability.
- **Worship and gratitude** — These displace fear and cultivate resilience.

Spiritual fitness isn't about hype—it's about endurance.
It's not about emotional zeal—it's about lasting strength.

Bearing Fruit Begins at the Root

Spiritual readiness isn't just about being alert—it's about being deeply anchored. When hardship hits, how do we respond with love, joy, peace, patience, kindness, goodness, faithfulness, gentleness, and self-control? Those aren't automatic reactions. They are the fruit of the Spirit (Galatians 5:22–23); and fruit doesn't appear without a healthy root system.

Jesus said, *"I am the vine, you are the branches. The one who remains in Me, and I in him, bears much fruit; for apart from Me you can do nothing."* (John 15:5)

Micah 6:8 reminds us what God desires: *"To do justice, to love kindness, and to walk humbly with your God."*

But how can we do justice or walk in humility if we're disconnected from the source? The more deeply we are rooted in Christ—through His Word, through prayer, through stillness in His presence—the more naturally His fruit is borne in our lives.

When storms come, it's the deep-rooted trees that remain standing. The remnant must not just be alert—we must be anchored.

Final Charge: Act Now

Don't wait for the storm—build your shelter before it hits.
Don't wait for the crisis—fast and pray now.
Don't wait for the fight—suit up today and every day.
Because when the trumpet sounds, it will be too late to lace up your boots.
And when the flames rise, it will be the prepared who lead the way.

So rise, remnant!

- Train like soldiers.
- Pray like warriors.
- Stand like saints.

14

Unshaken in a Shaking World

The world is trembling.
Kingdoms are toppling.
Foundations that once seemed secure are crumbling beneath our feet.
And yet, there remains a people who will not be moved.
The remnant.
Those anchored, not to earthly systems but to the Rock that cannot be shaken.
A Kingdom That Cannot Be Shaken.
The writer of Hebrews captures the spirit of this moment perfectly:

"Even then, his voice shook the earth; but now, he has made this promise:
'One more time I will shake not only the earth, but heaven too!'
And this phrase, 'one more time,' makes clear that the things shaken are removed, since they are created things,
so that the things not shaken may remain.
Therefore, since we have received an unshakeable Kingdom,
let us have grace, through which we may offer service that will please God, with reverence and fear. For indeed, "Our God is a consuming fire!"
— *Hebrews 12:26–29, (CJB)*

God is not surprised by the shaking. He ordained it. The shaking separates the true from the false. It exposes what's built on sand and reveals what's built on the Rock. For the remnant, the goal is not to cling harder to the old structures—it's to hold tighter to Christ Himself.

Biblical Examples of Unshaken Lives

Throughout Scripture, we see ordinary people standing unshaken in extraordinary times:

Elisha's Boldness:

When an enemy army surrounded his town, Elisha's servant panicked. But Elisha prayed, "Open his eyes, Lord, so that he may see" (**2 Kings 6:14–17, NLT**):

So one night the king of Aram sent a great army with many chariots and horses to surround the city.

When the servant of the man of God got up early the next morning and went outside, there were troops, horses, and chariots everywhere. "Oh, sir, what will we do now?" the young man cried to Elisha.

"Don't be afraid!" Elisha told him. "For there are more on our side than on theirs!" Then Elisha prayed, "O Lord, open his eyes and let him see!"

The Lord opened the young man's eyes, and when he looked up, he saw that the hillside around Elisha was filled with horses and chariots of fire.

Jael's Unexpected Victory:

While the mighty warriors of Israel hesitated, a housewife named Jael took decisive action. When the enemy, General Sisera, fled into her tent seeking refuge, Jael offered him milk, waited until he slept, and then drove a tent peg through his skull (Judges 4).

An unlikely hero, unshaken in a critical moment.

Jehoshaphat's Strategy:

Facing a vast enemy army, King Jehoshaphat didn't call for more weapons—he called for worship. As singers went ahead of the army, praising the beauty of God's holiness, the Lord set ambushes against their enemies (2 Chronicles 20:20–22, NLT):

Early the next morning the army of Judah went out into the wilderness of Tekoa. On the way Jehoshaphat stopped and said, "Listen to me, all you people of Judah and Jerusalem! Believe in the Lord your God, and you will be able to stand firm. Believe in his prophets, and you will succeed."

After consulting the people, the king appointed singers to walk ahead of the army, singing to the Lord and praising him for his holy splendor. This is what they sang:

"Give thanks to the Lord;
   his faithful love endures forever!"

At the very moment they began to sing and give praise, the Lord caused the armies of Ammon, Moab, and Mount Seir to start fighting among themselves.

Over and over, we see it:
Those who trust God stay anchored even when the earth quakes.

Modern Examples of Steadfast Faith

Corrie ten Boom

Corrie ten Boom, a Dutch watchmaker turned resistance hero, was arrested along with her family for hiding Jews during the Nazi occupation of the Netherlands. She was imprisoned in Ravensbrück, one of the most notorious women's concentration camps, where she witnessed unspeakable cruelty and watched her sister Betsie die from illness and abuse. And yet, through it all, Corrie clung to an unshakable hope in Christ.

She smuggled a Bible into the camp and held secret worship services in the barracks, bringing light into the darkest places. After the war, she traveled the world preaching forgiveness—even to some of her former captors. She later wrote, *"There is no pit so deep that God's love is not deeper still."* Her testimony still stirs hearts today as a living witness that no force on earth can shake the Kingdom of God in a soul fully surrendered.

Zev Porat

Born into a deeply Orthodox Jewish family in Israel, Zev Porat was the grandson of a prestigious rabbi and heir to significant family wealth. But everything changed when he had a supernatural encounter that led him to recognize Yeshua (Jesus) as the promised Messiah. His faith decision cost him dearly—he was shunned by his family and summoned to a lawyer's office, where he was told he could inherit millions in cash, property, and assets if he would only renounce Jesus.

Zev didn't flinch. He looked the attorney in the eye and said, "I will not deny Yeshua. You can keep the money." That courageous decision not only defined his life—it launched his ministry. Zev has since led many to faith in Yeshua through bold evangelism in the streets of Israel and abroad. He chose the riches of heaven over the wealth of man, and God has used him mightily in return.

Believers Under Persecution

Across the world, countless believers live out their faith under constant threat. In Iran, house churches meet in whispered secrecy behind locked doors. In North Korea, being caught with a Bible can mean torture or execution. In parts of Africa, entire Christian villages are attacked by militant extremists. And yet, these believers continue to worship.

They gather by candlelight, baptize in rivers under cover of night, and share the gospel at great personal risk. Their courage doesn't come from comfort—it comes from conviction. In every generation, the persecuted church reminds us that the gospel cannot be silenced, and the gates of hell will not prevail against it. These modern-day heroes stand unshaken, anchored in Christ, showing us what it truly means to overcome by the blood of the Lamb and the word of their testimony.

My Personal Shaking

I know what it's like to have your entire foundation collapse.

When I realized Mormonism wasn't the true Gospel, everything I believed, everything I lived for, suddenly felt like it was built on sand. It was terrifying. For a time, I didn't know what was real or whom to trust.

And yet—even in that season—I could not let go of the simple truth that

God is real, Jesus is real, and His plan for redemption is real. The enemy wanted me to throw everything away. But the Spirit whispered, *Stand*.

Even when you don't see clearly.
Even when you're trembling inside.
Hold your ground.

And that simple act of standing opened the door for God to rebuild my foundation—this time, on bedrock that could not be moved.

Sifted Like Wheat: Why God Allows the Shaking

"Simon, Simon, behold, Satan has demanded permission to sift you like wheat..."
(Luke 22:31)

Sifting isn't punishment—it's preparation. It separates the wheat from the chaff, the pure from the pretense. God allows it—not to break you, but to prove what's unshakable inside you.

When the enemy tries to shake your faith, God is refining it.

CLOSING CHARGE: STAND FIRM

You may not be able to stop the shaking—but you can choose where you stand. You can choose who you trust. You can choose whether to build your life on temporary systems—or on the eternal King.
Declare it today:
I will not be shaken.
I will not be moved.
I will stand on the Rock of Christ until the end.
No matter what crumbles around you—
Christ in you cannot be shaken.

Prayer of Declaration:

*Father, anchor my soul in You alone.
Teach me to stand firm when
the winds rage and the mountains tremble.
Let my trust be deeper than my fear.
Let my hope be higher than the storm.
You declared that no weapon formed
against me shall prosper.
So, I choose to build my life on the Rock
that cannot be moved.*
In Jesus' name, Amen.

15

Embracing Your Mission — Purpose in the Pressure

It's not an accident you're alive in this hour.
You were born for such a time as this.
You are not background noise.
You are not spiritual filler.
You are part of God's strategic plan to advance His Kingdom in the final days.
The remnant isn't called to retreat—we're called to engage.
Even if the world grows darker, even if the battle grows fiercer, the mission still remains: ***Shine. Stand. Speak. Serve.***

Every Believer Has a Unique Assignment

The Bible says we are Christ's body—many parts, different functions, but one Spirit.

> *"For we are His workmanship, created in Christ Jesus for good works, which God prepared beforehand so that we would walk in them."*
> *—Ephesians 2:10*

You don't have to be a preacher to be pivotal.
You don't have to be a prophet to be powerful.
You don't have to be a missionary to be missional.
Maybe your calling is to teach children the Word.
Maybe it's to encourage the weary.
Maybe it's to work quietly behind the scenes, strengthening others for the fight at hand.

Whatever your assignment is, it matters. The Kingdom of God advances through every act of obedience—large or small, seen or unseen.

You are not some haphazard mistake who just happened to be born. Scripture clearly teaches that God created you for a purpose. He has gifted you—both naturally and supernaturally—for your unique role in His Kingdom.

Hearing God's Call in Uncertain Times

How do you hear God's assignment for you?

Sometimes it comes as a burden—a holy discomfort about something broken that needs mending.

Sometimes it's revealed through the gifts and talents He's already placed inside you.

Sometimes it's through the prompting of His Spirit in prayer, or even through prophetic confirmation from trusted believers.

I once heard it said: "Your calling is where your deep gladness meets the world's deep need."

But calling also requires testing. Not every opportunity is an assignment. That's why cultivating prayer, Scripture knowledge, and discernment is crucial.

When in doubt, ask:

- Does this align with God's Word?
- Does this draw me closer to Christ?
- Does this serve others and glorify Him?

God rarely gives us the full map upfront. But He always lights the next step.

Hearing from God isn't reserved for an elite few. It's not a fringe experience. It's foundational. And it begins with learning to recognize His voice within. God doesn't speak to our brains; He speaks to our spirit. We must learn to trust the Holy Spirit within us—the still, small voice that confirms truth, reveals direction, and dispels confusion.

The spectacular can actually get in the way of the supernatural. We're often waiting for dramatic signs, when what we really need is a willingness to listen.

One word from God, whispered into the heart of a willing servant, can change everything. Consider Elijah, lodging in a cave, seeking the Lord, who said:

> *"Go out and stand on the mount before the Lord." And behold, the Lord passed by, and a great and strong wind tore the mountains and broke in pieces the rocks before the Lord, but the Lord was not in the wind. And after the wind an earthquake, but the Lord was not in the earthquake. And after the earthquake a fire, but the Lord was not in the fire. And after the fire the sound of a low whisper. And when Elijah heard it, he wrapped his face in his cloak and went out and stood at the entrance of the cave. And behold, there came a voice to him and said, "What are you doing here, Elijah?" (1 Kings 19:11–13).*

While God can and does speak in mighty ways, His voice usually comes to us as a gentle whisper.

IDENTIFYING YOUR PERSONAL ASSIGNMENT AND SPHERE OF INFLUENCE

HEARING GOD'S CALL
WHEN DISCERNING YOUR ASSIGNMENT, ASK:

- Does this align with God's Word?
- Does this draw me closer to Christ?
- Does this serve others and glorify Him?
- Does it bring peace, even if it challenges me?

Not everyone is called to the platform. Most of the Kingdom's battles are won in living rooms, classrooms, workplaces, and quiet daily obedience. Where has God placed you?

- Your neighborhood
- Your workplace
- Your online presence
- Your circle of influence

Ask Him to show you how to bloom where you're planted.
Your assignment might be raising godly children.
Or being a light to coworkers.

Or starting a Bible study.
Or writing a book that plants seeds for years to come.
Your life is not random.

The gifts you carry—natural and supernatural—have been entrusted to you by God. Some are woven into your DNA through your family line. Others are activated by the Holy Spirit after salvation. But all are meant for impact. Your natural abilities, talents, and skills that you develop are all components of your design and purpose. Nothing is too simple, nor too complex, for building the kingdom and the serving the body of believers.

God's assignments come in many forms: Through a sermon. A Scripture. A conversation. A sudden sense of clarity. Our job isn't to chase opportuny—it's to walk in step with the Spirit. Remember: Obedience is success, whether we understand the purpose or not.

> *Obedience isn't about having all the answers. It's about trusting the One who does.*

Biblical Examples of Obedience in Uncertainty

Abraham: Told to leave his country and family without knowing the destination.
He obeyed—and became the father of nations.

Ruth: A widowed foreigner who chose to stay with her grieving mother-in-law Naomi.
Her loyalty led to her becoming an ancestor of Jesus Himself.

Noah: Built a massive ark while everyone around him mocked and disbelieved. He obeyed—and preserved the human race.

Ananias: A little-known disciple tasked with laying hands on Saul—the persecutor of Christians—after his Damascus road encounter. Ananias was afraid, but he trusted the Lord and obeyed.

And Saul (his Hebrew name) became known as Paul, the apostle to the Gentiles.

How to Discern True Prophetic Confirmation

Sometimes God uses the body of Christ to confirm our callings. But how can you tell a true word from a false one?

Here are a few guideposts:

- ❖ It confirms, not confuses. A true prophetic word usually resonates with what God has already been stirring in your heart.
- ❖ It aligns with Scripture. God will never call you into sin, contradiction, or error.
- ❖ It bears good fruit. True words lead to faith, hope, repentance, or obedience—not fear, manipulation, or control.
- ❖ It brings peace. Even if the word challenges you, there's a deep, Holy Spirit peace attached to it.

God speaks from within—because that's where He lives. He will guide you through the witness of the Spirit, through peace or restraint, and through discernment that deepens over time.

You don't need a neon sign.

You need a soft heart tuned to His voice.

Personal Example:

During the COVID lockdowns, we were already feeling unsettled about staying in the home we loved. We had imagined we would stay in our home for many years to come, but deep in our spirits we felt we were supposed to move. We kept going back and forth—Is this the Lord or is it us? The Holy Spirit or the alarming events around the world that are making us feel unsettled?

After much prayer, we attended a special service where a visiting preacher was scheduled for three days of teaching and ministry. On the second evening, after the message, he came over to my husband and me and prophesied over us:

"The Lord says MOVE! And just to be perfectly clear—a geographical move!"

He went on to declare: "God is going to plant you in a fruitful vineyard."

We had never spoken to this preacher before—he knew nothing about our situation or the fact that we at had planned on growing grapes on three of our acres, but could not because the ground was heavy clay. And yet, the word he spoke was a clear confirmation of what we were already sensing.

It wasn't generic.

It wasn't manipulative.

It was precise.

And it bore good fruit.

God can and still does speak through others—but He also expects us to test everything to stay grounded in truth.

> "*Do not despise prophecies, but test all things;
> hold fast what is good.*"
> (1 Thessalonians 5:20–21)

Closing Charge: Step into Your Calling

The world doesn't need more spectators.
It needs Spirit-filled warriors walking in their assignments.
You don't have to have it all figured out.
You just have to say yes.
Because Heaven isn't looking for the perfect.
Heaven is looking for the willing.

Commissioning Prayer:

*Father, awaken in me the mission You crafted
before the foundation of the world.
Sharpen my hearing to recognize Your call.
Strengthen my heart to obey even when it costs.*

*Lead me to the people and places
You have assigned for this hour.*

*I say yes to Your Kingdom.
I say yes to Your call.
Here I am—send me.*
In Jesus' name, Amen.

16

THE WATCHMAN'S CRY

There are times when love looks like a warning.

To be a watchman is not to be paranoid or pessimistic—it's to be spiritually awake when others are asleep, to see from the wall what others can't see from the camp. And to have the courage to cry out, even when no one wants to hear it.

The remnant is being called into this role.

Not to incite fear, but to prepare hearts.

Not to condemn, but to call people higher.

Not to condemn. But to call.

WATCHMEN IN SCRIPTURE

God has always placed watchmen in His covenant community.

Ezekiel was appointed as one. The Lord told him, "Son of man, I have made you a watchman for the people of Israel; so hear the word I speak and give them warning from me" (Ezekiel 3:17). If he failed to sound the alarm, the blood would be on his hands.

Jeremiah wept as he warned. His heart was broken for the nation, but his warnings were largely ignored—until judgment came.

Isaiah wrote of watchmen who see the messenger running with good news. Not every message is a rebuke or a warning—sometimes it's a shout of hope.

"How beautiful on the mountains are the feet of those who bring good news." (Isaiah 52:7–8).

And then there's **Mordecai**, an unexpected watchman. While serving in the king's court, he overheard a plot to assassinate the king and took action. His vigilance saved lives and later positioned him to help save an entire people group.

New Testament Watchmen

The role of the watchman didn't vanish in the New Testament. It was simply reshaped through the lens of Christ.

In Acts 11, a prophet named Agabus stood up and *"predicted by the Spirit that a great famine would spread over the entire Roman world." (Acts 11:28)*

The church listened—and took action.

They didn't argue about conspiracy theories.

They didn't bury their heads in the sand.

They prepared—generously, practically, and in unity.

The same is true for us. The Spirit is still speaking today. The watchmen are still watching. But will the people listen?

The apostle Paul also stood in the role of a watchman. In 2 Timothy 3:1–13, he gave Timothy—and the entire church—a stark warning about the Last Days:

> *"But understand this, that in the last days there will come times of difficulty. For people will be lovers of self, lovers of money, proud, arrogant, abusive, disobedient to their parents, ungrateful, unholy, heartless, unappeasable, slanderous, without self-control, brutal, not loving good, treacherous, reckless, swollen with conceit, lovers of pleasure rather than lovers of God, having the appearance of godliness, but denying its power" (vv. 1–5, ESV)*

Paul didn't sugarcoat the truth.

He didn't try to be politically correct.

He issued a call to clarity, courage, and discernment.

"Evil men and impostors will go from bad to worse, deceiving and being deceived. But as for you, continue in what you have learned…" (vv. 13–14)

Paul was sounding the alarm—not just for Timothy, but for the Church across all generations.

He saw what was coming.

He warned boldly.

And he charged believers to stand firm in truth, even as deception increased.

The baton is now in our hands.

The Watchman's Cry

A Watchman in American History

Sometimes God places a watchman not on a wall—but on a midnight horse.

On the night of April 18, 1775, Paul Revere rode through the darkness to warn of advancing British troops. But contrary to the simplified grade school version, he wasn't acting alone. Revere was just one part of a much larger alert system—a network of watchmen.

The Sons of Liberty had prepared a warning strategy. When British troop movements were spotted, Revere had a friend place two lanterns in the steeple of Christ Church (now known as the Old North Church). It was a coded signal: the Redcoats were coming by sea.

But it didn't stop there.

Patriots across the Charles River saw the signal and sprang into action. Revere himself was one of at least three riders—possibly five—who spread the warning that night. Together, their efforts mobilized the militias and alerted the towns that would soon face the battles of Lexington and Concord.

It wasn't just one man's courage.

It was a remnant working together to sound the alarm.

What if Revere had stayed silent?

What if the others hadn't lit the lanterns… or taken up the ride… or paid attention to the signal?

That same question echoes today.

What if we stay silent?

Now is the time for modern-day watchmen—Spirit-filled, truth-bearing believers—to take up the cry.

It may not be a midnight ride. It may not be a steeple lantern. But it is just as urgent. And it still takes all of us.

What If the Watchman Warns, but No One Listens?

Sounding the alarm is only half the equation.

The other half is whether the people listen.

History is filled with moments when warnings were sounded—clearly, urgently, even prophetically—but were ignored. The cost of ignoring the watchman is often catastrophic.

Pearl Harbor (1941)

In the days leading up to December 7, intelligence sources warned that Japan was planning something big. Three days before the attack, intercepted communications suggested an imminent threat—but the information was dismissed, downplayed, or lost in bureaucratic inertia.

Even on the morning of the attack, radar operators saw incoming aircraft and sounded the alarm. It was brushed off as a scheduled flight of American B-17s.

The result? Over 2,400 Americans died. The Pacific Fleet was devastated. America was thrust into World War II.

How different things may have turned out had the warnings been heeded!

The Challenger Disaster (1986)

The night before NASA's Challenger space shuttle launch, engineers from Morton Thiokol warned that the O-rings on the rocket boosters could fail in cold temperatures. They pleaded for a delay. Their advice was ignored—brushed aside by deadlines, pressure, and pride.

Seventy-three seconds after takeoff, the shuttle exploded. Seven astronauts perished. The tragedy shook the nation. The science was sound. The warning was clear. But decision-makers didn't listen.

THREE WARNINGS. THREE OUTCOMES. ONE PATTERN.

The radar was ignored at Pearl Harbor.
The engineers were silenced before Challenger.
The prophetic warning of Jesus was heard—and heeded—by a faithful remnant.
History has spoken. Will we listen?
These stories may come from different eras, but the message is timeless:
The responsibility of the watchman is to warn.
The responsibility of the people is to respond.
Today's Church faces the same dilemma. Will we heed the spiritual radar? Or will we dismiss the warnings as too radical, too inconvenient, too uncomfortable?

Truth doesn't wait for consensus. And obedience doesn't require full understanding—just faith and readiness.

"If the trumpet gives an uncertain sound, who shall prepare himself to the battle?"—1 Corinthians 14:8 (KJV)

The Fall of Jerusalem (70 A.D.)

Jesus Himself gave a clear prophetic warning: *"Not one stone here will be left on another; every one will be thrown down." —Matthew 24:2*

Decades before it happened, He warned His followers to flee the city when they saw Jerusalem surrounded by armies (Luke 21:20–21). Many early Christians heeded that prophetic word and escaped to safety. But those who didn't perished in one of the most brutal sieges in history.

The Messiah gave the warning. The remnant responded. And their obedience spared them.

How to Sound the Alarm Without Turning People Off

Being a watchman is not about shouting louder than everyone else. It's about speaking with clarity, love, and conviction—even if your voice shakes.

Yes, there are strange and catastrophic things ahead—Scripture says men's hearts will fail them for fear of what's coming on the earth (Luke 21:26). Spiritual warfare. Global shaking. Demonic deception dressed up as aliens or Nephilim reborn. The remnant isn't called to panic. **We're called to anchor deep**.

If our warnings sound like Henny Penny ("the sky is falling!") or the boy who cried wolf, people will tune us out—even when the danger is real.

It's hard enough to get people to store some food, keep cash on hand, or pack a "go bag" without being called paranoid.

So how do we sound the alarm about the unthinkable without coming across as unhinged? Here's how the remnant can do it well:

> **Pray before you speak.** Make sure the warning comes from the Spirit, not from fear or frustration.

> **Avoid sensationalism.** Speak with sober urgency, not shock value. Truth doesn't need theatrics to be powerful. It needs conviction, not performance.

Not every warning has to be loud.

The most powerful watchmen are not the most dramatic— they're the most discerning.

Clarity over chaos. Conviction over volume. Anchored—not alarmist.

- ➤ **Use discernment in timing.** Not every truth needs to be spoken immediately—or publicly. Ask, "Is this the right time? The right setting?"
- ➤ **Speak the truth in love** (Ephesians 4:15). Warnings without love feel like condemnation. Love without truth offers false comfort.
- ➤ **Let peace anchor your tone.** If what you're saying causes confusion or panic, ask the Lord to help you reframe it. The Holy Spirit brings conviction, not chaos.
- ➤ **Be ready for rejection.** Not everyone will listen. That doesn't mean you failed—it means they still have a choice.

Because here's the truth:
Our responsibility is to warn. Theirs is to respond.
But let's make sure when we speak, it sounds like Jesus—not a doomsday prophet with a bullhorn.
The goal of a watchman isn't to be right.
It's to be faithful.

THE ULTIMATE WARNING: ETERNITY IS AT STAKE

As watchmen, we warn about coming trouble—spiritual deception, societal collapse, natural disasters, even demonic manifestations. But there's one warning that far outweighs them all:
Hell is real. And judgment is coming.
What benefit is it to store food, build a bunker, or survive global upheaval—if the soul is still lost?
Jesus asked it plainly:

> *"What good will it be for someone to gain the whole world, yet forfeit their soul?" —Matthew 16:26*

There is no greater danger than entering eternity unprepared.

> *"Just as it is appointed for man to die once, and after that comes judgment,*
> *so Christ, having been offered once to bear the sins of many,*
> *will appear a second time, not to deal with sin*
> *but to save those who are eagerly waiting for him."*
> *—Hebrews 9:27–28*

*The greatest danger isn't what's coming to earth.
It's what comes after death.*

Every person has an appointment with death.
There are no second chances after we die.
Only in this life can we repent, receive Christ, and be made new.
So while we must be faithful to warn of what's coming on the earth—
we must never forget to warn of what's coming after it.
Eternity is real.
Judgment is certain.
And Jesus is the only escape.
If we fail to say that, we've failed in the most important watchman duty of all.

Final Charge: Rise and Cry Out

If God has given you vision, If He has stirred you with urgency, If you see what others cannot—don't silence yourself.
The enemy would love nothing more than to mute the messengers of God. But this is the hour for truth to be proclaimed, even in the wilderness. Even if they roll their eyes, call you "*too intense*," or walk away—be faithful.
Blow the trumpet.
Sound the alarm.
Lift your voice.
Because someone will hear.
Someone will repent.
Someone will be saved.
And even if they don't—at least the warning was given.

*When the world stops listening,
the faithful remnant rises.*

Commissioning Prayer

Lord, make us faithful watchmen.
Give us eyes to see what You are revealing,
Ears to hear Your Spirit's whisper,
And courage to speak what must be spoken.

When others sleep, keep us alert.
When others mock, make us bold.
When fear tempts us to stay silent,
Remind us that love tells the truth.

Let us sound the alarm—not to condemn,
But to call people into Your mercy
Before the shaking comes.
Use our voices to awaken hearts.
Use our warnings to prepare the way.
Use our lives as a beacon on the wall.
In Jesus' name, Amen.

SITUATIONAL AWARENESS CHECKLIST

Living alert, not afraid, wise as serpents, innocent as doves (Matthew 10:16)

PHYSICAL AWARENESS — "EYES OPEN, HEAD UP"

❏ I locate at least two exits when entering a new building or public space.

❏ I avoid being glued to my phone in unfamiliar places.

❏ I observe body language and stay alert to signs of nervousness or suspicious behavior.

❏ I listen to the Holy Spirit and my instincts when something feels "off."

❏ I carry permitted protective items (e.g., pepper spray, flashlight, whistle, or legal concealed weapon).

❏ I avoid drawing attention to myself in volatile areas unless led by the Spirit.

MENTAL AWARENESS — "STAY SHARP"

❏ I regularly ask myself: If something happened right now, what would I do?

❏ I stay alert by limiting distractions like headphones or deep daydreaming in public spaces.

❏ I stay informed on current events without letting fear take root.

❏ I have a clear family emergency plan for communication breakdowns.

SPIRITUAL AWARENESS — "EYES TO SEE, EARS TO HEAR"

❏ I pray before I go out, asking God for discernment, protection, and divine appointments.

❏ I respond when the Holy Spirit prompts me to change course or delay.

❏ I regularly pray over my loved ones, coworkers, and community.

❏ I stay rooted in Scripture to sharpen my discernment and remember God's promises.

❏ I speak God's truth aloud as a declaration of faith and spiritual authority.

Preparedness Basics — "Ready Without Paranoia"

❏ I keep a 'go bag' with water, snacks, flashlight, battery pack, and basic first aid items.

❏ I know basic self-defense or first aid techniques.

❏ I keep a small amount of cash on hand in case of emergency.

❏ I have digital and physical backups of important documents.

❏ I practice staying calm in crisis--prepared to help others, not just myself.

❏ I choose to live alert but not afraid--anchored in faith, led by the Spirit, and prepared to stand.

Check off what you can.
Pray over what you can't.
But don't go back to sleep.

∞

Pause and Reflect
One habit I've allowed to slip? Is there one area I've overlooked?
Lord, show me where I need sharper awareness.

Eyes Open ✦ Mind Ready ✦ Spirit Anchored ✦ Feet Prepared

17

Community in the Wilderness — Finding Strength in the Few

There's a kind of loneliness only the remnant understands. It's not just being physically alone—it's carrying convictions that the wider culture rejects. It's holding fast to truth when even your brothers and sisters in Christ sometimes turn away. It's walking through the wilderness seasons when it feels like the crowd is thinning, and the familiar structures are crumbling.

And yet... you are not alone.

Simulated Connection vs. Spirit-Led Covenant

In today's world, technology can simulate conversation, but it cannot create true connection. Social media promises friendship, but often delivers loneliness. AI can mirror your words, but it cannot mirror your soul. We were created for something deeper. God designed us for presence, vulnerability, truth, and covenant relationships—connections rooted not just in shared interests, but in shared lives and Spirit-led love.

(Part 1 of 2 – continued next page)

> *(Part 2 of 2 – from previous page)*
>
> As artificial companionship becomes more common, the remnant must guard against trading safe simulations for sacred relationships. True fellowship requires patience. It requires risk. It requires the Spirit of God moving between hearts. In the days ahead, people will be desperate for something real.
> **We must be the ones who offer it.**

TECHNOLOGY CAN SIMULATE CONVERSATION.
ONLY THE SPIRIT CAN FORGE COVENANT.

BIBLICAL AND HISTORICAL EXAMPLES OF FAITHFUL FELLOWSHIP

In every era of redemptive history, God has preserved a faithful few—and often, they found one another:

- ❖ Elijah thought he was the only one left who hadn't bowed to Baal. But God told him there were 7,000 others. Hidden, yes—but not alone.
- ❖ David was driven into the wilderness by Saul, yet surrounded by his "mighty men;" loyal companions who risked their lives to stand with him—their leader and friend.
- ❖ Paul often traveled with trusted co-laborers like Barnabas, Silas, and Timothy. He longed for fellowship and found strength in the spiritual family he established.
- ❖ In more recent history, figures like Corrie Ten Boom and Brother Andrew—founder of Open Doors—drew encouragement from tight-knit bands of believers as they resisted darkness and brought light behind enemy lines.

The "desert places" may feel empty; but often, it's where the most meaningful bonds are formed.

You may feel isolated—but you're not alone.
God has preserved others who have not bowed.

Navigating the Pain of Church Wounds

Let's be honest—some of us feel like we've been exiled. Not by geography, but by rejection. By legalism. By betrayal. Church wounds are real. And Scripture doesn't gloss over them.

- David was hunted by his spiritual leader, Saul.
- Jesus was betrayed by Judas—one of the twelve.
- Paul was abandoned and opposed by those he once trusted (2 Timothy 4:10, 14).
- The Galatians were "bewitched" into legalism and turned cold toward Paul for a time.

It happens. Maybe it happened to you. Maybe a leader dismissed your calling. Perhaps your church didn't understand your hunger for Scriptural truth. Maybe you were labeled as divisive for simply pursuing more. But hear this, wounding is not the end of your story.

> *God sees your pain. And He hasn't left you wandering. He's leading you into fellowship that will heal— not harm.*

Healing After the Hurt

Healing doesn't mean pretending it didn't hurt.

Healing doesn't mean rushing back into unsafe relationships.

Healing means allowing the Spirit to wash the wounds with truth, to rebuild trust slowly, and to lead you into new relationships where iron can truly and wisely sharpen iron.

Remember: even after Judas, Jesus didn't stop forming covenant relationships.

Even after betrayals, Paul kept pouring his life into others.

Forgiveness frees you even when others don't repent.

Wisdom teaches you how to discern, how to set boundaries, and how to connect again without falling into old patterns of harm.

Healing is messy.

Healing is slow.

But healing is holy.

True Fellowship vs. Performance Religion

The remnant must reject surface-level religion. We don't need more polished small groups that avoid the hard conversations. We don't need fellowship halls filled with hidden bitterness and plastered smiles. We need communities built on the Spirit of truth, humility, and love.

Acts 2:42 paints the picture: *"They devoted themselves to the apostles' teaching and to fellowship, to the breaking of bread and to prayer."*

It wasn't about programs or polish. It was about breaking bread together—sharing life in real time. It was about prayer and devotion and holding one another up in a hostile world. The remnant must be determined to build that kind of fellowship again.

Yes, it will be messy.

Yes, it will require forgiveness and grace.

Yes, it will be worth it.

Because in the wilderness, fellowship isn't just a nice addition. It's survival.

Creating Fellowship That Goes Beyond the Walls

Church doesn't have to look like pews and pulpits. In fact, some of the most powerful expressions of body life happen around kitchen tables and campfires.

> *"They devoted themselves to the apostles' teaching and to fellowship, to the breaking of bread and to prayer."* —Acts 2:42

In the early church:

- They met house to house.
- They shared meals.
- They prayed and prophesied together.
- They faced persecution side by side.

It wasn't about convenience. It was covenant. You can cultivate that, too:

➤ Start a discipleship trio with two trusted friends.

➤ Form a watch group that discerns current events through Scripture.

➤ Launch a "tentmaker team" with a shared mission or outreach.

Whatever it looks like—just start. Because in the wilderness, a fire burns brighter when others are gathered around it.

How to Find and Foster Remnant Community

You don't need a megachurch to find kingdom fellowship. You need:

- Truth in common
- Faith on fire
- Love without compromise

Start where you are. Ask the Lord to highlight people who carry that same Spirit-driven hunger. It might be a neighbor, a coworker, a homeschooling parent, or a fellow online believer.

Here are some practical ways to begin:

➤ Host a simple prayer gathering in your home.

➤ Start a small study group focused on discernment and end-times readiness.

➤ Attend or initiate a local worship night.

➤ Use platforms like Telegram, Zoom, or Signal to stay connected.

➤ Never underestimate the power of one-on-one fellowship. Jesus discipled twelve—but He also poured into individuals.

Wherever two or more are gathered in His name, He is there.
Matthew 18:20

Final Charge

If you've been hurt—heal.
If you've been isolated—rebuild.
If you've been disappointed—hope again.
The remnant is rising not just as individuals—but as a body.
We need each other.

Prayer for the Hurting Remnant

*Father, bind up the brokenhearted
among Your remnant.
Heal the wounds inflicted by brothers,
leaders, and friends who failed us.
Soften hearts that have grown cold in isolation.
Rekindle trust where betrayal once burned.*

*Teach us to build covenant community—
not through performance, but through Your Spirit.
Connect us with the right people
in the right time, for the right purpose.*

*We declare that loneliness will not define us.
Isolation will not imprison us.
Fear will not rule us.*

*We are the body of Christ,
joined together by love and truth.*
In Jesus' name, Amen.

18

Living Ready: Hope, Holiness, and the Return of the King

The remnant must be many things in this hour.
Courageous.
Discerning.
Rooted in the Word.
Alive in the Spirit.
But above all, we must be a people anchored in hope—a hope that fuels holy living as we wait for the return of our true King.
Because what we believe about the future directly impacts how we live today.

Hope as a Weapon

Hope is not passive.
It's not wishful thinking.
It's not naive optimism.
Hope is a weapon forged in the fires of God's promises.
Hope reminds us that no matter how dark the world gets, the Light has already overcome.

Hope reminds us that no matter how fierce the battle, the victory has already been won. The enemy works overtime to rob believers of hope. Because a hopeless Christian is an ineffective Christian.

But the remnant refuses to let go.

We hope because we have seen His faithfulness in the past.

We hope because the tomb is still empty.

We hope because the King is still coming.

Hope keeps our lamps burning while the night grows dark.

How to Live in Hope Daily

So how do we live as hope-bearers when the world is crumbling? Here are a few practical ways:

- **Stay in the Word.** Romans 15:4 reminds us that the Scriptures were written to give us endurance and encouragement so that we might have hope.
- **Pray with expectation.** Even if the answer hasn't come yet, pray like the answer is on the way.
- **Testify of His goodness.** Share what God has done in your life. Hope grows when we remember.
- **Worship before the breakthrough.** Praise Him not just for what He's done, but for who He is.
- **Encourage others.** Sometimes the hope we give away is the hope we get back. Anchor yourself in knowing God's character—that He is good and His plan for you outlasts the current circumstances.

Holiness: The Garment of Readiness

Hope and holiness are woven together. Peter writes:

"Therefore, preparing your minds for action, be sober-minded; set your hope fully on the grace that will be brought to you at the revelation of Jesus Christ. As obedient children, do not be conformed to the passions of your former ignorance, but as He who called you is holy, you also be holy in all your conduct." — 1 Peter 1:13–15

Holiness isn't legalism—it's readiness.
It's the wedding garment we prepare for the Bridegroom's return.
It's the oil in our lamps when the midnight cry rings out.
Holiness doesn't mean perfection, it means devotion..
It's staying awake when the world is asleep.
It's choosing the narrow road when the broad road beckons.
It's keeping our hearts pure—not to earn His love, but because we already have it.

THE TIME IS NOW

There are moments in history when the winds shift—when something deeper than cultural trends begins to stir. We are in such a moment now.

- ❖ *Bible sales are rising.*
- ❖ Campuses are erupting in spontaneous worship.
- ❖ Young people are hungry for truth—not sugar-coated, not watered down, but real, raw, Spirit-breathed truth.

This isn't coincidence. It's kingdom momentum, and momentum demands movement.

The remnant isn't meant to just survive these days—we're meant to ignite them.

We can't afford to hesitate, overthink, or retreat into passivity. This is a strike-while-the-iron's-hot moment. A shout-it-from-the-rooftops hour.

The Lord is drawing hearts, preparing minds, and He's looking for messengers who will rise up with the Word in their mouths and fire in their bones.

The harvest is not coming—it's here.

The fields are not barren—they're bursting.

The Mission Until He Comes

Hope fuels holiness.
Holiness fuels mission.
We're not called to bunker down and wait for rescue. We're called to occupy until He comes. Jesus said:

> "You are the light of the world. A city set on a hill cannot be hidden."— Matthew 5:14

Our job is to keep shining.
To keep sowing seeds. To keep watching, warning, loving, praying, and preaching.
Because every act of faithfulness today ripples into eternity.

> **Now is the Time to Preach.**
> **Now is the Time to Write.**
> **Now is the Time to Move.**
> ♦
> **The remnant must rise.**

Your Mission is Now

You were born for this time.
You were placed on earth in this generation for a purpose.
You are not an accident.
2 Corinthians 5:18–20 reminds us:

> "God…gave us the ministry of reconciliation…Therefore, we are ambassadors for Christ, God making his appeal through us."

You are not a spectator—you are an ambassador.
An ambassador is not sent to stay silent.
An ambassador speaks on behalf of the King.
An ambassador defends the values of the kingdom they represent.
You are deployed on earth for divine diplomacy. In fact, you've been appointed for a special assignment to modern-day Babylon. Don't bury your commission under busyness or fear.
The time is now.

You carry the culture of heaven into the chaos of earth.

Reflection:

The world will grow darker.
But the light in the remnant will grow brighter.
The harvest will grow heavier.
But the laborers must grow stronger.
The King is coming.
Will He find us ready?

Prayer:

Father, awaken our hearts to hope.
Anchor our lives in holiness.
Ignite our hands for mission.

May we be found faithful—burning bright in the night, fearless in the battle, unwavering in the waiting.
We will not shrink back.
We will not grow cold.
We refuse to be silent.

Strengthen Your remnant.
Equip Your watchmen.
Deploy Your ambassadors.

Until the skies split and the trumpet sounds—
We will stand. We will shine. We will proclaim.
In Jesus' name, Amen.

REMNANT RISING

19

Embracing Reluctant Obedience

When we picture the remnant rising boldly in the last days, we sometimes imagine a fearless, unwavering army—marching forward without hesitation.
But the truth is, many of God's greatest warriors started out reluctant.
Obedience doesn't always begin with enthusiasm.
Sometimes it begins with trembling hands, pounding hearts, and whispered prayers of "Lord, are You sure?"
The important thing is not whether we feel afraid or unqualified.
It's whether we choose to say yes anyway.

Biblical Examples of Reluctant Obedience

The Bible is filled with stories of people who wrestled with God's call before submitting to it:

- **Moses** — When God called Moses to confront Pharaoh, Moses protested: "Who am I that I should go?" (Exodus 3:11). He argued. He pleaded. He begged God to send someone else. And yet, despite his fear and insecurity, he went—and God used him to deliver a nation.

- **Gideon** — When the angel of the Lord appeared to Gideon and called him a "mighty man of valor," Gideon was hiding in a winepress. He doubted his own strength. He questioned God's presence. But in the end, he trusted; and through him God defeated an army with only 300 men.

- **Ezekiel** — Called to a difficult prophetic ministry, Ezekiel balked when God instructed him to bake bread over human dung as a sign to Israel. (Ezekiel 4:12–15). He cried out in distress—and God mercifully allowed a substitution. Obedience didn't mean the absence of discomfort; it meant willingness to follow through even when the assignment was hard.

- **Jonah** — Jonah literally ran the other way when God told him to preach to Nineveh. His reluctance was fueled by fear and prejudice. Yet God, in His mercy, pursued Jonah, redirected him, and still used him to spark one of the greatest revivals recorded in Scripture.

- **Ananias (in Acts 9)** — When the Lord told Ananias to go pray for Saul (later Paul), Ananias protested: "Lord, I have heard from many about this man, how much harm he did to Your saints..." (Acts 9:13). But despite his fear, Ananias obeyed—and God used him to restore Saul's sight and launch one of the most powerful ministries in church history.

- **Peter** — Even after receiving visions from heaven, Peter hesitated to associate with Gentiles. But God rebuked his bias, and Peter eventually crossed the threshold into Cornelius's house—opening the door for the gospel to spread to all nations (Acts 10).

Historical Echoes: Reluctant Yet Mighty

Throughout history, we see echoes of reluctant obedience that shaped the course of nations:

- **George Washington** — Initially reluctant to lead, Washington accepted the call to command the Continental Army during the American Revolution. Later, he hesitated to become the first President of the United States, but answered the call nonetheless—laying the foundation for democratic leadership.

- **Corrie ten Boom** — After surviving the horrors of a Nazi concentration camp, Corrie wrestled deeply with forgiving her captors. It didn't come easily. It wasn't automatic. But by the grace of God, she obeyed the call to forgive—and her testimony has inspired millions around the world.

- ❖ **Dietrich Bonhoeffer** — A brilliant German theologian, Bonhoeffer struggled with his role in resisting the Nazi regime. Pacifism and theology collided with political reality, and his decision to join a plot to stop Hitler cost him his life. His reluctant but resolute obedience still stirs the global Church with the cost of true discipleship.
- ❖ **Harriet Tubman** — Born into slavery, Tubman escaped to freedom but felt God calling her back—again and again—to rescue others. She admitted to fear, illness, and doubt, but she pressed on in obedience, leading over 70 enslaved people to freedom via the Underground Railroad. Her quiet, trembling "yes" changed history.

Encouragement for Today

If you feel reluctant, you are not disqualified.
If you feel afraid, you are not disqualified.
If you wrestle with the cost, you are not disqualified.
God is not looking for flawless volunteers.
He is looking for surrendered vessels.

God's Power Perfected in Weakness

You are not called because you are fearless.
You are not chosen because you are confident.
You are called because He is faithful—and His strength is made perfect in weakness.
Remember Paul's words:

"But He said to me, 'My grace is sufficient for you, for My power is made perfect in weakness.' Therefore I will boast all the more gladly about my weaknesses, so that Christ's power may rest on me."
— *2 Corinthians 12:9*

The remnant isn't made up of superheroes.
It's made up of surrendered sons and daughters.

Jesus told a parable of two sons in Matthew 21:28–32. One son refused his father's command but later obeyed. The other son agreed with words but disobeyed in action. The one who ultimately obeyed was the one commended.

Attitude matters, but action matters more.

> *God can work with reluctant obedience.*
> *He cannot work with hardened rebellion.*

Your Reluctance Can Become Your Testimony

One day, your story might sound like this:
"I didn't feel ready... but I obeyed anyway.
I didn't feel strong... but I obeyed anyway.
I didn't know the outcome... but I trusted anyway."

The world needs real testimonies—stories of people who followed God through fear, through trembling, and through uncertainty.

Not flawless people. Faithful ones.

Commissioning Prayer

Father, we come with our fear.
We come with our doubts.
We come with our trembling hearts.
And we lay them at Your feet.

Give us the courage to say yes
even when we're scared.
Give us the strength to obey
even when we feel unqualified.
Give us the faith to trust
even when the way is unclear.

Like Moses, Gideon, Jonah, Ananias, and Peter—
Use us in spite of our reluctance.
Transform our weakness into Your testimony.
We say today, not in our own strength
but by Your Spirit:
"Here am I, Lord. Send me."
In Jesus' name, Amen.

Remnant Rising

20

FINAL WORDS FOR THE FAITHFUL

We are not waiting for the battle to begin—we are in it. And the remnant has been placed here on purpose. This is not the hour to sleep. This is not the time to shrink back, make peace with passivity, or bow to cultural compromise. You were not refined just to survive. You were refined to rise.

The world is shaking. Deception is deepening. Evil no longer hides in shadows—it marches in parades. The prophets of this age aren't calling down fire; they're calling good evil and evil good. Truth has become offensive. Compromise is considered love. And silence is celebrated as wisdom.

But the remnant knows better. We were warned:

"There will be terrible times in the last days."

Men will be lovers of self. Truth will be traded for lies.

False signs and wonders will deceive even the elect—if that were possible.

This is not fiction.

This is not fear-mongering.

This is the Word of God—and it's unfolding in real time.

The shaking you feel? That's not failure. That's alignment. That's the sound of the King preparing His people. Not for retreat—but for impact.

You Were Born for Battle

The same Spirit that empowered Elijah, emboldened Esther, and sustained Stephen is alive in you. You may feel small, unseen, disqualified, weary—but you were chosen for this hour. You are not here by accident.

You carry the fire of heaven in a jar of clay—and it was never about your strength. It was always about His glory.

Let the world mock. Let Babylon rage. Let the false prophets speak smooth words to itching ears.

The remnant must speak truth—loudly when needed, quietly when led, but always without compromise.

Don't water down your witness to stay liked.

Do not trade eternal truth for temporary applause.

Do not exchange your assignment for an easier path.

Watchmen, Warriors, Witnesses

You are a watchman. You see what others ignore.
You are a warrior. You battle what others deny.
You are a witness. You testify to what others forget.

And the time has come—not to blend in, but to break forth.

The trumpet is sounding.
Not a cultural call. Not a political cause.
A Kingdom call—to rise, to stand, to go.

Commissioning Charge

This is your moment, remnant.
Not to become famous, but to become faithful.
Not to build platforms, but to prepare paths.
Not to hoard comfort, but to carry light.

You were refined in private.
You were tested in silence.
Now rise with resolve.

Go where He sends you.
Say what He gives you.
Stand where others fall away.

You were not called to be clever. You were called to be courageous.
You were not called to be liked. You were called to be light.
You were not called to echo the world. You were called to disrupt it with truth.
You were not just *born again*.
You were born *for this*.

Prayer of Commission

Father God,
We hear the trumpet. We see the signs.
We feel the shaking.
And still—we say yes.
Yes to the call.
Yes to the fire.
Yes to the assignment.

Make us faithful. Make us fearless.
Set our feet like flint and our eyes on eternity.
Strengthen our arms for battle and our hearts for obedience.

Let us not fear the darkness—let us carry the light.
Let us not retreat from culture—let us redeem it.
Let us not shrink back in silence—let us speak with holy fire.
You are our strength. You are our banner.
We are Yours.
In Jesus' name, Amen.

> But we are not of those who shrink back
> and are destroyed,
> but of those who believe
> and are saved.
> —Hebrews 10:39

◆ ◆ ◆

Remnant Ready

Spirit Led

Fearless

◆ ◆ ◆

Author Note
From One Watchman to Another

If you've made it to this final page, then I believe you're part of the remnant—those God has awakened for such a time as this.

You've felt the shaking. You've heard the whisper. You've counted the cost. And still… you've said yes.

I didn't write this book as someone with all the answers. I wrote it as a sister in the trenches—a remnant believer who has wrestled, wept, and wondered whether faithful obedience to the call would truly make a difference.

What I can tell you is this: God sees the ones who won't bow. He marks those who refuse to blend in. And He strengthens the ones who feel weak but still say, "Here I am. Send me."

You are not alone. You were never forgotten. And your assignment is not small in the eyes of heaven.

The faithful will rise from hidden places.
Voices will cry out in the wilderness.
Oil will be found in unexpected lamps.
And the roar of the Lion will reverberate through the universe
when He returns for His bride.
Keep standing. Keep shining. Keep speaking.
We were born for this.

With love and resolve,

Tracy Tennant

Fellow Watchman, Sister in the Battle

Appendix A
Scripture Verses for the Remnant

When the world shakes, the Word stands.
Come back to these verses often.

Strength & Endurance

- Isaiah 40:31
- Galatians 6:9
- Hebrews 12:1-3
- 2 Timothy 4:7-8
- James 1:12
- Philippians 4:13
- 2 Corinthians 12:9
- Psalm 28:7
- Psalm 46:1
- Nehemiah 8:10

Discernment & Wisdom

- James 1:5
- Proverbs 3:5-6
- 1 Kings 3:9
- Hebrews 5:14
- 1 John 4:1
- Romans 12:2
- Matthew 7:24
- Proverbs 4:7
- Proverbs 1:5
- Psalm 119:66

Boldness and Courage

- Acts 4:29-31
- Joshua 1:9
- Deuteronomy 31:6
- Proverbs 28:1
- Psalm 56:3-4
- 1 Corinthians 16:13
- Psalm 27:14
- Isaiah 41:10
- 1 Chronicles 28:20
- Ephesians 6:10

Faithfulness & Obedience

- John 14:15
- Luke 16:10
- 1 Corinthians 4:2
- Deuteronomy 5:33
- Matthew 7:21
- 1 Samuel 15:22
- Philippians 2:8
- James 4:7
- Exodus 19:5
- Romans 12:11

Continued: Scripture Verses or the Remnant

Hope & Promise

- Jeremiah 29:11
- Romans 15:13
- Revelation 21:4
- Titus 2:13
- Isaiah 43:2
- 1 Corinthians 2:9
- 2 Corinthians 4:16-18
- Hebrews 11:1
- Philippians 1:6
- Romans 8:28

Identity & Calling

- Jeremiah 1:5
- Ephesians 2:10
- 1 Peter 2:9
- Galatians 2:20
- Romans 11:29
- Psalm 139:14
- Romans 8:16-17
- 2 Corinthians 5:17
- 2 Timothy 1:9
- Mark 16:15

*These are verses to equip, encourage, and anchor you
in your mission as a remnant believer.
Memorize them.
Meditate on them.
Carry them into battle.*

Appendix B

Endnotes and References

This appendix provides references, credits, and source notes for quotations, stories, Scripture citations, and historical details referenced throughout *Remnant Rising: Standing Unshaken in a Shaken World*.

Scripture References

All Scripture quotations are taken from the New American Standard Bible (NASB) unless otherwise noted.

Verses are cited in-text throughout the chapters for immediate clarity and accessibility.

Historical and Cultural References

NASA. *"Near Miss: The Solar Superstorm of July 2012."* Accessed May 2, 2025. https://science.nasa.gov/science-research/planetary-science/23jul_superstorm/.

Ten Boom, Corrie. *The Hiding Place.* New York: Bantam, 1971.

Porat, Zev. *Unmasking the Chaldean Spirit.* 2021.

Metaxas, Eric. *Amazing Grace: William Wilberforce and the Heroic Campaign to End Slavery.* New York: HarperOne, 2007.

Elliot, Elisabeth. *A Chance to Die: The Life and Legacy of Amy Carmichael.* Grand Rapids, MI: Revell, 1987.

Heiser, Michael S. *The Unseen Realm: Recovering the Supernatural Worldview of the Bible.* Bellingham, WA: Lexham Press, 2015.

AI and Technology Disclaimers

MIT Technology Review. "*Deepfake Scam Cons Victim out of $243,000.*" Accessed May 2, 2025. https://www.technologyreview.com.

All That's Interesting. "*Project Blue Beam and Alien Deception Theories.*" Accessed May 2, 2025. https://allthatsinteresting.com/project-blue-beam.

Neuralink. "*Brain-Machine Interface Technology.*" Neuralink Blog. Accessed May 2, 2025. https://www.neuralink.com/blog.

OpenAI. "*AI Safety and Deception Safeguards.*" Accessed May 2, 2025. https://openai.com/safety.

Space Safety Magazine. "*Missed Warnings: The Fatal Flaws Which Doomed Challenger.*" Accessed May 2, 2025. https://www.spacesafetymagazine.com/space-disasters/challenger-disaster/missed-warnings-fatal-flaws-doomed-challenger/.

National WWII Museum. "*The Three Missed Tactical Warnings That Could Have Made a Difference at Pearl Harbor.*" Accessed May 2, 2025. https://www.nationalww2museum.org/war/articles/pearl-harbor-missed-tactical-warnings.

Ten Boom, Corrie. Quote on Chinese bishop and persecution. Anecdotal and widely circulated in Christian teaching; verify against public speeches or interviews.

Pull-Quotes, Insert Sources, and Special Mentions

Pull-quotes were created based on thematic content drawn from the main text or restated Scripture insights.

The 'More Than Eden' reflection is inspired by theological frameworks introduced in *The Unseen Realm* by Dr. Michael S. Heiser.

Ministry and Resource Citations

Book recommendations listed in Appendix D are independently selected by the author based on their contribution to building discernment, endurance, and spiritual maturity.

Appendix B

No financial affiliation, sponsorship, or compensation exists between the author and recommended ministries, books, podcasts, or organizations.

Important Note

Every effort was made to ensure accuracy, honor source material, and maintain integrity throughout this book.

If a quote, idea, or reference significantly shaped part of the content, credit has been given here or in the body text.

Any similarities to other works are purely coincidental and unintentional. This project was created with a sincere desire to inform, encourage, and equip the remnant Body of Christ.

Appendix C

How to Start a Remnant Group

In times of shaking, isolation can be dangerous. God designed the remnant not to be scattered survivors, but to be a network of courageous believers strengthening each other for the days ahead.

If you feel the stirring to start a small fellowship, prayer group, or Bible study, here's how to begin:

1. **Pray for Discernment and Direction**

    - Ask the Holy Spirit if He is calling you to initiate a group.
    - Pray for wisdom about when, where, and how often to meet.
    - Seek His leading regarding who to invite.

2. **Start with a Few**

    - You don't need a large number to begin. Jesus said, "Where two or three are gathered in My name, there am I among them" (Matthew 18:20).
    - Invite trusted friends, family members, or believers you sense are hungry for deeper fellowship and truth.

3. **Establish Purpose and Vision**

    - Clarify the purpose: Is it a Bible study? A prayer group? Fellowship and encouragement?
    - Share the vision from the beginning so everyone so everyone is clear on the heart and purpose of the gathering.

- Choose a Format that Fits
- Home gatherings, rotating host homes, outdoor meetups, Zoom or other video conference platforms (if in-person isn't possibley).
- Keep it simple. It's about connection, not performance.

Example flow:
- **Open with prayer.**
- **Share a short Scripture, teaching, or discussion prompt.**
- **Allow open conversation, sharing, and testimonies.**
- **Close with prayer and any practical needs or next steps.**

4. **Foster an Atmosphere of Authenticity**
   - Encourage honesty and humility.
   - Remind participants: This is not a place for performance—it's a place for strengthening.
   - Be prepared for messiness. Real life is messy, but God meets us there.

5. **Stay Grounded in the Word and Spirit**
   - Keep Scripture central to your gatherings.
   - Prioritize prayer. Don't let it become an afterthought.
   - Allow space for the Holy Spirit to move through worship, prayer, prophetic encouragement, and discernment.

6. **Expect Resistance—and Press On**
   - When believers gather with genuine hunger, the enemy notices.
   - Expect distractions, discouragements, and even misunderstandings.
   - Stay humble, stay loving, and keep your eyes on Jesus.

Appendix C

Closing Thought

You don't need a title. You don't need a microphone. You just need a willing heart.

The early church changed the world—one house at a time. The remnant can, too.

"And they devoted themselves to the apostles' teaching and the fellowship, to the breaking of bread and the prayers."
—Acts 2:42

Appendix D

Recommended Resources for the Remnant

Here are trusted books, ministries, and other tools selected for their contribution to spiritual maturity, biblical understanding, and equipping the Body of Christ for times of shaking. Each one is included to help strengthen and prepare you for the days ahead.

Books

- *Supernatural* — Michael S. Heiser
- *The Bible Unfiltered* — Michael S. Heiser
- *The Kingdom Priesthood* — Dr. Michael Lake
- *The Insanity of God* — Nik Ripken
- *Live Not by Lies* — Rod Dreher
- *The Hiding Place* — Corrie ten Boom
- *Omega Dynamics* — Jamie Walden

Podcasts and Sermon Series

- Kingdom Intelligence Briefing (Podcasts to empower the remnant)
- VOM Radio (Voice of the Martyrs)
- The Remnant Radio (theology, discernment, Spirit-led living)
- Holy Ghost Stories (Bible stories told beautifully)
- 66/40 with Chuck Missler (Comprehensive Bible study)
- Kolob to Calvary (faith transition, truth, and remnant equipping)

Ministries and Missions Organizations

- ➤ Voice of the Martyrs (persecuted church advocacy)
- ➤ Open Doors USA (supporting persecuted believers)
- ➤ One for Israel (Messianic Jewish outreach)
- ➤ Global Catalytic Ministries (underground church movements)

Online Tools and Resources

- ➤ Blue Letter Bible (deep Bible study tools, lexicon, cross-references)
- ➤ Bible Gateway (multiple translations, topical searches)
- ➤ Logos Bible Software (advanced Bible study, scholarly resources, original texts)

> Always test everything by Scripture and prayer.
> Even trusted voices can get it wrong—so stay anchored in the Word and led by the Spirit.

Closing Note

There's a flood of content out there.
Choose carefully.
Test everything against the Word and Spirit.
Build your faith on what endures.
The remnant must not only stand—we must grow strong.

"Let the Word of Christ dwell in you richly."
—Colossians 3:16

✦ Chosen. Anchored. Equipped ✦

Other Works by the Author

Books

The Warrior's Walk:
Keys to Victory in Spiritual Battle
Inspirational dive into the armor of God.

Mormonism, the Matrix, and Me:
My Journey from Kolob to Calvary
Details Tracy's spiritual journey out of Mormonism into biblical faith.

Confessions of an Ex-Mormon:
What I Wish I Knew When I Left the Church
A guide to navigating the transition out of the LDS faith.

Confessions of an Ex-Mormon Recovery Journal
Self-guided journal to process the journey out of Mormonism.

No Excuses Reading Journals
Self-guided reading journals to keep track of the books
you read and keep notes on them. For various book genres.

Websites

TheMormonMatrix.com
TracyTennant.com

Other

Listen to her podcast *From Kolob to Calvary,*
available on iTunes and other platforms.

To contact the author, send email to:
TracyTennant@outlook.com

www.ingramcontent.com/pod-product-compliance
Lightning Source LLC
Chambersburg PA
CBHW070105080526
44586CB00013B/1188